INTO UNCERTAINTY

Sometimes you just have to take the leap

WAYNE DOUGLAS HARRISON

INTO
UNCERTAINTY

Sometimes you just have to take the leap

WAYNE DOUGLAS HARRISON

The **Journeys of Courage** Series
by **Wayne Douglas Harrison**

Out of Fear
2nd Edition Release – December, 2021

Into Uncertainty
2nd Edition Release – December, 2021

Taking Control
2nd Edition Release – December, 2021

Making a Difference
Coming 2022

Available on **www.brainspiredpublishing.com**,
as well as bookstores and online shopping
around the world.

The **Journeys of Courage** Series
Into Uncertainty by Wayne Douglas Harrison
2nd Edition

Cover design by *Bridget McGale*
McGale & Associates, Saint John, New Brunswick, Canada

To contact Wayne Douglas Harrison
authorwaynedouglasharrison@gmail.com
Visit my website at **www.authorwaynedouglasharrison.com**

Brainspired Publishing
A joint venture of Brainchild Holdings Inc. and INspired Media Inc.

Brainspired Publishing
Ontario, Canada
www.brainspiredpublishing.com

PAPERBACK ISBN: 978-1-7774054-9-6
Library and Archives Canada / Government of Canada

For our grandchildren (in birth order)
David, Emma, Carter, Hailey, and Link.
May you always experience unconditional love.

INTO UNCERTAINTY

Sometimes you just have to take the leap

The Journeys of Courage series

INTO
UNCERTAINTY

"Sometimes you just have to take the leap"

The Journey of Courage series

Chapter 1

The Matheson house took on air of desolation as the sound of the slammed door resonated into a long, empty pause. Martha looked at her husband, Grant, and started sobbing. The loud, wet, and ugly kind of sob where the face contorts into shapes and colours no one ever thought were even possible.

Grant stood in seething anger with his taut face several shades beyond deep red.

Mackenzie wondered if her father was on the verge of blowing an artery. She stood there stunned trying to digest all that had happened. Her brother, Brock, had, just minutes before, come out at his eighteenth birthday party and their father told him he was not welcome in their home and that he was dead to him before kicking him out of the house. Her mother's silent agreement exposed her bigotry as she stood by without saying a word. The worst-case scenario she and her brother had imagined had happened.

She had a questioning look that bounced between her parents before exclaiming, "What parenting guru told you that throwing your child out of his home is the mark of a great parent? Brock lived his life out of fear that this would happen one day but we both hoped you loved him enough to support him. I guess not. I really thought you two were better than this."

Her father interrupted and tersely responded, "Don't disrespect your parents!"

Her face erupted into full colour as she thrust the palm of her hand in front of his face, "Just stop!" Her exasperation was in full force as she stepped forward to stand face-to-face challenging his power and locked her eyes on his, "Right now I'm having a hard time thinking of something to respect. All I have to say to you both about what has happened tonight is ………. REALLY?" She flew out of the room and up the stairs.

*****

Brock walked out onto the driveway and headed for Mahogany Manor Bed & Breakfast where he worked. The gay couple who owned '*the Manor*', Andrew Wallace and Gregory Allen, had offered their home as a safe place for him to fall in the event his parents kicked him out. As he walked, the crunch of the snow awakened his focused mind and he pulled out his phone.

Andrew and Gregory wondered aloud about how Brock was doing when Andrew's phone sounded. They saw it was Brock and breathed a sigh of relief though it was short lived when they heard his sobs. They couldn't make out a word he had said but they knew it wasn't good. Andrew asked, "Where are you now, we will come and get you?"

Brock's "Not far, I'll be there shortly" response was laboured but clear.

"We are here for you." was all Andrew could add.

Brock made his way to '*the Manor*' through tears that almost blinded him. He had made a New Year's resolution eight days ago to come out to his homophobic father and subservient mother on his eighteenth birthday. He knew it could go badly but he decided he was done being dishonest trying to live his life to please others.

Andrew and Gregory waited in the foyer turret windows and when they saw Brock come into view, they went out onto the verandah. Brock climbed the stairs and collapsed, sobbing into Gregory's arms. Gregory struggled to hold this man, who was six inches taller and 60 pounds heavier, draped over his body. Andrew supported them both from behind Gregory and whispered soothing words into Brock's ear. The sobs subsided and he regained some control. They helped him into the house and back into the kitchen where they seated him. He was defeated but collected himself and told them what they had already guessed.

Brock detailed the evening and quoted his father's hurtful words: '*As long as you insist on being gay, you are dead to me. I do not want you as my son and you are no longer welcome in my home. Get out!*' When Brock said the '*dead to me*' statement, the guys looked at each other remorsefully knowing that those words would be burned onto his psyche for the rest of his life.

Brock, looking up at them, asked, "Are you sure it's okay for me to live here. If it isn't..."

Andrew interrupted him, "Brock, we are absolutely sure."

They calmed him down. He was an exhausted, emotional mess.

Mammie's ring tone sounded. Brock knew she would be concerned, so he took the call. She was his next-door neighbour whom he had grown up with and he felt like she was more a grandmother than a neighbour. "Hi Mammie."

Her normally sweet voice had an edge to it as she asked, "Honey, are you okay?"

"Mammie, the worst has happened, they kicked me out. I'm at '*the Manor*' now." Brock broke down again.

She heard his anguish and explained, "I was passing through my dining room and saw the glow of the candles on your cake as your mother brought it in to you with Mackenzie following. I saw their mouths going and it looked so wonderful that I stood there and sang along with them. I watched as you concentrated before you blew the candles out and I could almost hear your silent words making that special wish. When you cut the cake and passed the pieces around, I felt I was sitting at the table with you. I felt so happy for you, but then the scene changed. You weren't eating your cake and I could sense the turmoil you were feeling.

The happy occasion then turned into something that was anything but happy. I could only guess the worst. I felt guilty for intruding, but I was transfixed and needed to support you. You seemed so lost. Then your father and mother said something to you, and you stood. I saw the anger in your face, and you had, what looked like, terse words with them. I do not know what was said, but I saw you punch the wall and then leave your home. I went to the front window to wave, but you were so focused and direct in your walk that you didn't look up. You looked like you were crying. That is when I knew, for sure, that the worst had happened.

I wanted to reach out to you but waited because I didn't want to interfere. I couldn't wait any longer. Honey, I'm sick about what I saw, and I'm so concerned that I needed to call you. Can you come here so we can talk?"

The realization hit him that she was party to what had happened. She could guess but didn't really know all the details. She was concerned and needed to see him. She meant so much to him, so ignoring his emotional exhaustion he cautioned, "It's getting late. I'm concerned about you getting your sleep."

She broke in, "What I saw tonight will haunt me until I know, so I won't be sleeping. Please come."

"Okay, I'll be there in ten minutes. I'll use the front door so I have less of a chance that I'll run into my parents."

"Okay Honey, do be careful; the sidewalk looks icy."

"They are icy, but I will be careful."

He explained to Andrew and Gregory that he needed to go talk to Mammie. They hugged him, wished him well, and watched as he walked away with slumped shoulders and hands shoved deep into his pockets. They were both thinking of the unfortunate turn of events that this night had brought.

Chapter 2

On his way, he called his best friend, Matthew, to tell him how the night had gone. He broke down as he relived what had happened. He told him he was on his way to see Mammie.

"I'll come over too; I don't want you to be alone." Matthew's concern was etched into his words.

"No, I'll be okay but thanks. You need to get your sleep and I need to spend some time with Mammie. Then, I need to return to '*the Manor*' to get some sleep, if that's even possible. I'll talk with you tomorrow."

"Are you sure you don't want some moral support?"

"Thanks, but I'm having a hard time processing all that was said, and I need to get my head around it. Sleep well, good night!"

Brock's thoughts were whizzing through his brain as he relived his birthday party and he concerned himself with the unknown future he was now facing. No matter how much planning he had done, now that he was kicked out, his life seemed bleak. Although he couldn't articulate it at that moment, when he would tell others about what he felt, he would say he understood what people meant when they said they couldn't think straight. He was on autopilot and got to Mammie's home without remembering any details of the actual journey.

When he realized he was in front of her home, he looked up and saw her in the doorway. At the same time, he took a sideways glance at his home, or what used to be his home. Everything looked the same, almost as if tonight hadn't really happened. It felt like he was in a bad dream and the realization that he wasn't welcome there hit him hard.

Mammie saw Brock look at his home and knew the pain he was feeling. When he stepped inside, she clung to him with a strength that he never knew she had. He wrapped his arms around her trying to capture as much of her love as he could; he needed this right now more than anything else. As they stood in each other's arms, he broke and started sobbing; a keening, wracking, snotty surrender. He tried to take control several times but just when he told himself that he was done, his body would erupt in yet another wave. He needed the release and could do nothing but go along for the emotional ride.

His upheaval subsided and when he quieted, he released her. He realized his tears drenched the top of her blouse and that he needed to blow his nose. He reached into his pocket and pulled out a useless, soggy ball of used tissues. Mammie passed him a box that had been sitting on the side table. He created a fortified shield of several tissues and blew so hard he wondered if they would be able to contain it. He took more and wiped his swollen eyes; they were so sore. "I'm so sorry that you had to see this."

"Don't ever be ashamed of showing emotions. A good cry is cleansing for the soul. Let's go sit on the couch. I made us some hot chocolate."

Brock took off his coat, moved into the living room, and sat down. As he sipped his drink, he savoured how soothing it was. He wished he could crawl into the cup, curl up, and be enveloped by the warmth. "I feel bad that you saw the fight and that it caused you concern."

"Don't be. I feel embarrassed that I was an accidental, but willing, voyeur in such a private situation but my concern for you was larger than my embarrassment. I need to know what happened, but only if you feel comfortable telling me. I do not want to push even though that's what I feel I've done so far."

"Mammie, I would share anything with you. You have always provided a safe and loving place for me. This has been a horrible day and I'm glad I visited you before going home. Your love helped me through tonight. Having had the worst happen has devastated me beyond anything I had expected. I thought I was prepared, but I guess there was a part of me that expected my parents to love me more than they do. I was so wrong and now I feel lost. I now know that whatever they were feeling that caused them to kick me out is stronger than their love for me."

"I love you more than I could love anyone, and I will help you in whatever way you need. I know I'm not your parent, but I feel like a close second. I lost one son and I want you in my life until the day I die."

"I can't get Dad's words out of my head. When he kicked me out, he told me I was no longer his son and that I was dead to him." He watched her face as the horror of his father's words sank in.

"Oh Honey, those are awful words. The only thing I can hope is that they were said in the fit of emotion. I hope he will see the error of his ways and reconsider tomorrow. Let's see what tomorrow will bring. Remember, I would love to have you move in here with me when you're ready to be living next door to your parents."

"Thank you, Mammie, you're so sweet, but this is just too close and I'm too raw right now to even think about it. I hope you're right about tomorrow, but I can't imagine how someone could simply take those words back. I'm blessed to have such wonderful people in my life who will support me through this turmoil." He went on to explain that in anticipating his father's reaction, he had secretly moved the important things that he would need to '*the Manor*' a bit at a time over the past week. Mackenzie agreed to retrieve anything he hadn't taken and deliver it to him. All he had to do was text her.

"I have known I am gay for awhile, but I stayed '*in the closet*' with Mom and Dad out of fear that I would lose all the people I loved. I got so tired of not being honest with myself and the people I loved that it became too much for me, so I made the decision to come out. I wish my parents responded like you had. What is wrong with them?"

"A wise person once gave me a gift of wisdom and I think you might appreciate it today. '*It is unfair to judge others because their journeys are different than our own.*' Remember what we talked about that day in the garden. We are all on journeys of learning as we evolve to be our best selves. Each of us is on that journey, but it's hard to expect all people to evolve at the same pace in the same time frame. Your parents are on their journeys and they are evolving differently than you. Age has nothing to do with it."

"How did you become so wise?"

"I've had some difficult lessons in life and there were times I didn't understand what I was supposed to learn. Out of each difficulty in my life that I experienced, came some learning. When I met Benny, my parents didn't like him because he was French, Catholic, and working class. In their eyes he wasn't good enough for their daughter and forbade me to see him. Not seeing him became too much for me, so I went against their wishes and concocted ways we could be together. One day Father caught us out at a restaurant, and he flew into a rage. He dragged me out of the place, took me home, and within a day I was sent to live with my aunt in Boston. It all happened so fast; I couldn't tell Benny. I thought my life was over."

Brock encouraged her to continue, "How long did you stay in Boston?"

"A shorter time than I thought I would. You see, I had grown close to Mary, one of our maids. We were like sisters although we couldn't behave that way when Father was at home. When Father sent me away, she missed me terribly and thought about Benny not knowing. She had gone into my mother's address book while she was out one day and got my aunt's address in Boston. She sent it to Benny at his place of work and told him what had happened to me.

Benny knew how strict Father was and he figured that my aunt would intercept any letters to me so the only way to contact me was in person. He took some time off and within a week he was on the train to Boston. One afternoon, I was sitting in my bedroom on the second floor looking out my window at the park across the street. I was so sad and spent many hours thinking of Benny while I looked out that window. One day, I thought my eyes were playing a trick on me because I thought I saw Benny waving his arms in the park. It was him! I was overjoyed and wrote him a note. I dropped it out the window and it fluttered into the street. In it, I told him I would try to run an errand and, for him to meet me two corners down.

My aunt was pleased that I had left my bedroom and suggested I go outside to get some air. I gladly went and we met at the corner. When Benny saw me, he blurted out, 'Will you marry me?'

I didn't have to think long. "Yes, but how?"

He had done some preliminary planning, so he knew what we needed to do. He even had bought me this ring."

She showed Brock a simple gold band on her ring finger. "We didn't want to chance something happening, so we laid out our plans. Benny set it up and I agreed to meet him on that corner at ten o'clock the next morning. I knew my Aunt was going to be out until suppertime, so I planned a walk. We were married just shortly after ten thirty and had a wonderful celebratory lunch at a dingy little restaurant I knew my aunt wouldn't frequent. Afterward, I mailed my aunt a note so she wouldn't worry. We then boarded the ship back to Saint John and I figured that by the time my aunt got the note, I would be well on my way home.

We arrived to find my parents and sisters at the passenger dock. My aunt had called them that morning after reading my note and my father was determined he was going to take me home. Benny stepped in front of me as Father reached for my arm and showed him the marriage certificate. Father tried to snatch it from him, but Benny withdrew it before it could be taken. Father gave me an ultimatum of annulling the marriage or I would no longer be part of his family.

I chose Benny and told my family that our home would always be open to them if they changed their minds. Father forbade me to have any contact with any of them. I have a bit of a stubborn streak in me and I told him we would make a life without him if that was his wish. That was the last time I saw them. They all died in a car accident months later." She paused.

After a minute of silence, she continued, "People think they are doing the right thing when they make those ultimatums, but that can be misguided and could be doing more harm than good. I'm so sorry you had to witness your parents' inability to see through their prejudice to the pure love you have for them. My hope is they do their work and realize what they have lost. I believe you are an instrument to help them learn." She paused and then continued,

"I missed my family terribly over those months before the car accident took them away forever, but I didn't attempt to contact them. I let my pride blind me and I was as pig-headed as my father. I believed Mother would have tried to contact me, but Father ruled that household, and, in hindsight, I now know Mother wouldn't have crossed him. Father's prejudice has caused me a lot of heartache over the course of my life when there really was no need; life is too short. Brock, it really doesn't matter what difference causes families to divide, but it happens when people cannot see beyond their prejudice. I hope you're not so proud or stubborn to miss any opportunity to reconnect with your family. I know they love you; they just have a funny way of showing it right now."

"I didn't realize you suffered this way."

"We all have our lessons; some really easy, but many of them are difficult." She took his hand in hers and assured him, "Never doubt that my home is your home anytime you want to be here. I love you."

"Thank you, you do not know how much I needed to hear that right now." She was still holding his hand when he looked her in the eyes. The second they connected he felt her love and compassion course throughout his body. "I'm so glad you're in my life!"

"And I'm glad you're in mine!"

"I had better get back to 'the Manor'; they are probably waiting up for me. It's so nice to have wonderful people supporting me!"

He put his coat on and they walked to the door. "I'm going to miss seeing you every day when you leave your home. Please plan some visits so we don't lose touch."

"Oh, Mammie, I promise to visit regularly." He hugged her and kissed her cheek. He noticed again that she was getting so frail and that worried him. "Call me anytime; I love to hear your voice."

Chapter 3

When he got back to '*the Manor*', the guys were waiting up for him. He filled them in on what had happened when he met Mammie and the story she told. They were impressed with Mammie's foresight and compassion.

Brock got to bed by midnight, but he didn't sleep much. Without really wanting to, he rolled the day's events over and over in his mind. When the sun rose around eight o'clock, he couldn't discern if he had gotten any sleep at all; his head ached, his limbs were heavy, and his eyes burned. He lay there looking at the ceiling imagining what was going on at home. As if he was being controlled by an unknown entity, he rolled over, got to his knees and started pummeling his pillow, first slowly, but then faster and harder, until he erupted into a sobbing mess. He jammed his face into the pillow to muffle the sound.

Andrew and Gregory were walking by the staircase leading to Brock's room when they heard the muffled noises and knew he was in pain. They looked at each other, and each gave a slight slow shake of the head before continuing downstairs to the kitchen.

Brock called Matthew to let him know he was okay and after ending the call, he dressed and went downstairs. There hadn't been any guests last evening so when he walked in the kitchen, he wasn't surprised to find the guys sitting at the table in pyjama pants and t-shirts. Andrew even had bedhead. He greeted them, "Good morning guys."

"Hi, Brock". They couldn't say good morning and mean it after last night. Andrew continued, "How are you doing? Did you get any sleep?"

"Not much but I think I now know what it feels like to be run over by a truck! Yesterday was a big day, some bad, some good, but if Mammie is right, it all is part of my learning. Why do lessons have to be so hard?"

"Some of our most valuable learning comes from some of the hardest lessons. As a good friend of mine often says; '*Nothing worthwhile comes easily*.'." Gregory offered.

The doorbell rang and the guys looked at each other and Andrew asked, "I didn't think we were expecting anyone this morning. Brock, we are not dressed to greet guests, would you mind getting the door?"

Brock went out and they could hear voices. He popped his head in the kitchen, "Mackenzie just arrived; do you mind if she joins us?"

The guys were relieved, and Gregory responded, "Bring her in!"

She walked in and took a seat as if she owned the place. She looked the guys up and down and sassed, "Aren't we casual today? I like the look!"

The guys guffawed and Andrew commented, "Aren't you just the fashion critic?"

"Someone has got to be. Andrew, did you think to look in a mirror? That hair is screaming for a good brushing!" Mackenzie laughed and took Brock along with her. "It's good to see you laugh after last night's fiasco. Mom told me this morning that she was looking out last night hoping to see you return home and saw you leaving Mrs. DesRoches' place about eleven o'clock. What were you doing there?"

He explained her call and his subsequent visit. He filled her in on the Mammie's personal rejection story and the wisdom she shared. "I just love that woman more than I ever thought possible."

"What a sad story; I mean her personal rejection story. She lost her whole family twice in one year!" She looked thoughtful for a moment and gave her assessment of what was said, "I guess just because a person is old, doesn't mean they are narrow in their views. Now that I say that, I think I have always prejudged her. Well, I need to give my head a slap."

"Here, let me help you." Andrew reached over and made like he was about to slap her.

Mackenzie glared at him, "I would think twice about going through with that if I were you '*Mr. Bedhead*'."

They all laughed again.

She looked at Brock, "I brought a load of the things you had listed when we were doing our planning. Now you have almost everything here that's important to you."

"Almost, what do you mean by that? What did I not put on that list?"

"Me!"

More laughter and when it subsided, Brock asked, "How were Mom and Dad this morning?"

"Mom looked like she hadn't slept a wink and, by the time I left, Dad hadn't come out of the bedroom."

"Did Mom know those things you took were for me?"

"Yes, I made sure she knew, just to rub it in. I also told her I was taking them to you in your new home at Mahogany Manor." She looked at Andrew and Gregory and switched gears, "I have been thinking a lot about what happened, and I want Mom to attend the next Pflag meeting. She needs to be in a room with other parents so she can ask the questions that Dad can't answer. She's a smart woman who does stupid things under Dad's influence. The meeting is next Friday the fifteenth, being the third Friday; Right?"

Andrew answered, "You're correct and I hope you can get her there. I suppose it is crazy to think you might encourage your dad to attend too. Your whole family needs what Pflag can offer right now."

"I would be more than pleased if that would happen, but I won't be holding my breath. She looked at Brock and asked, "Are you okay not going to the meeting? If Mom agrees to go, I need you to not be there until she is ready."

Brock didn't even have to think about it, "I would love it if you could get Mom there so whatever you need me to do!"

*****

Throughout Saturday and Sunday, Brock tried to busy himself around the B&B only to discover he was staring at a wall, out a window, at a picture, or at nothing and when he snapped back into reality, he realized he had been thinking about his life. Mammie's suggestion that his father would come around and take back his hateful words didn't materialize and, even though he didn't think it was possible, he sank deeper into his emotional void.

Matthew visited both days and tried to lift his spirits, but Brock was steadfast in mourning the life he knew before he was kicked out of his home. He couldn't shake his feelings of loss and his energy level plummeted.

Chapter 4

Brock awoke on Monday and, although it was familiar to him, it felt foreign to be thinking about getting up and going to school from '*the Manor*'. He lay there looking at the ceiling and thinking about all that had happened since he left school on Friday and reflected on how fast things can change. He rolled out of bed and went to take a shower.

Andrew was in the kitchen when Brock walked in. "Good morning, did you get any sleep?"

"I'm feeling dazed, but I would say I'm okay. I hadn't slept much Saturday night, but I died when my head hit the pillow last night. It just feels a little weird to be going to school from here."

"Change is always something we need to get used to." Andrew said as he finished making some of the breakfast items. "Would you like breakfast?"

Just then, the doorbell rang, and Gregory called from somewhere, "I'll get that."

Brock looked at the food, "You know, I think I would like some. When I got up, the idea of eating nauseated me, but the smells in here are intoxicating and I think my stomach has overridden my head." He grabbed a plate and was spooning on some scrambled eggs when he heard someone walk in. He turned expecting Gregory but got a surprise.

Matthew followed as Gregory walked in announcing, "Look who I found at the door."

Brock smiled, "What a pleasant surprise having you drop in."

Matthew winked at Brock and looked at his plate of food, "Doesn't that look good. Is there enough for an unexpected visitor?"

They all laughed, and Andrew responded, "For you, always! Grab a plate and help yourself."

All four took food to the table. Gregory looked around and smiled. "I'm glad the guest decided to eat a bit later today. This way we can eat as a family before the kids go off to school."

Brock looked at Matthew, "We've made family status. Does this mean you're now my brother?"

"I like the idea of being family, but I want to be more than just your brother so let's not go there. Anyway, I thought I would just alter my path a little this morning and walk to school with you. That's okay, isn't it?"

"It's perfect. I didn't want to walk to school by myself and you showing up takes the edge off that concern." Brock reached over and placed his hand on top of Matthew's and gave it a little squeeze.

Andrew queried, "What is causing you hesitation? Are you concerned students will see you leaving here and ask you why?"

Brock looked uncertain, "Yeah, I guess. I really don't want anyone to know what happened. It's funny that coming out of the closet has put me in another closet about living here. Everything is all linked together, and I'm just not ready to come out at school. Maybe I won't have a choice, but I'm not looking forward to finding out."

After breakfast, Matthew and Brock were hesitating by the front door, looking out the windows. Gregory understood what they were doing. "You two just hold your head high and walk out there as if you do not have a care in the world and no one will really notice. If they do and they ask, tell them it was about your work. It isn't a lie because you probably wouldn't be living here if you weren't working for us. Once you give that excuse, you need not tell them anything else."

Brock thought through Gregory's convoluted logic, "OK, if you say so." They said their goodbyes and left. Not a soul was on Germain Street, so they decided to walk out to Duke Street and down to the school.

The walk was without incident and when they arrived at the school Kyle popped out of the throng of students. "Did you guys take a different route today? I was waiting in Queen's Square, but when you didn't show, I left so I wouldn't be late."

Brock considered Gregory's answer, but didn't use it when he responded. "Yes, we decided to see a different street."

Kyle nodded, "I do that all the time. Going the same way can be boring at times. The reason I wanted to talk was that I heard from Trevor over the weekend. He's still in Boston and doing very well. I asked if he remembered you from 'the Manor' and said some really nice things about you. I guess you two hit it off."

Brock listened while his sweat glands activated as fear engulfed him. Not knowing what Kyle knew ate away at his confidence, but he hung on to the trust he had in Trevor. He had to believe that even though Kyle and Trevor were friends, Trevor wouldn't break his promise and divulge his secret.

Kyle continued, "He is coming up for his mom and dad's twenty-fifth anniversary next month. I believe it is on Saturday, the 27th. I suggested we all go out for supper. Would you be up for that?"

Brock panicked, "That would be fun, but I'm not sure I'll be available because of work, but thanks for asking."

Kyle was excited and didn't see a problem, "Trevor would have stayed with us, but since my grandmother moved in, we don't have a spare room. He says he booked a room at Mahogany Manor, so you'll probably see him there anyway. Maybe you can work something out with the guys so you'll be free for supper one night. We have almost a month to plan."

Kyle seemed to have a solution for every situation and wouldn't take 'no' for an answer. Brock was feeling like he was stuck in a corner. On one side he would love to see Trevor again, but on the other he wondered what Trevor and Kyle had discussed about him. "Okay Kyle, let me talk to the guys and find out what the schedule looks like. I'll do what I can."

"Great! See you later." Kyle walked off about six feet before turning around and giving a little salute.

This whole time Matthew was watching and had so many questions. "Who is Trevor and why are you freaking out?"

Brock tried to remember what he had told Matthew. "Remember I told you about having my first time with a guest at 'the Manor' last summer, well that guy was Trevor."

A smug look of realization washed across Matthew's face. "And Trevor is Kyle's friend, so you're freaking out because you're afraid Kyle knows. Am I right?"

"Bingo. I trust that Trevor wouldn't have said anything, but there is the possibility. Now, Kyle hasn't teased me, and I would expect he would if he knew, so that's a positive. Maybe Trevor isn't out to Kyle. Then again, I just don't know."

The day at school was arduous and Brock was so relieved when the last bell rang. He and Matthew walked up to 'the Manor'. Andrew and Gregory were in the kitchen and he told them about the conversation he had with Kyle about Trevor.

Andrew confirmed that Trevor had called that afternoon and asked if they had a room for the nights of February 26th to the 28th. "He normally would have stayed in the room you now have, so I booked him in one of our other rooms; at no charge of course; unless you would like him to stay in your room." He winked as he finished the suggestion.

Matthew had a response to Andrew's attempt at humour, "Not unless I get to stay as well! Wouldn't that be fun!"

All three shot him a shocked look.

"Gotcha!" Matthew exclaimed and looked quite pleased with himself.

They all laughed at his quick wit.

Brock marvelled at Matthew's ability to joke in a carefree manner and decided to play along. "Come here, dude." He raised one arm and slid it around Matthew's shoulder as if he were going to hug him but continued right into a headlock and held him there. "That will teach you to play games on us! Say 'uncle' and I'll release you!"

"I'm kinda liking this closeness. I could really use a little attention after all the stress of this weird day. Should we go upstairs?"

Brock broke out into laughter and let him go. He shook his head at his crazy friend and said, "Wouldn't you just love that!"

Chapter 5

Alice ran her finger down the page of the phone book and dialled the number. The phone was answered on the fourth ring. "Hello."

"Can I speak to Wade Jackson?"

"Speaking."

"My name is Alice DesRoches and we met while you were looking after Sally Beaumont's affairs. She was my cousin, and I was impressed with how you handled everything for her."

"That's kind of you to say, thank you. I believe I remember meeting you at Caring Hearts Hospice during Sally's stay there and again at her funeral. It's not that I have a great memory, more that she had such a small family."

"I'm glad you remember. I'm wondering if you would be my representative like you were for Sally. I need an executor for my will and someone to be my Power of Attorney and Medical Power of Attorney. I will pay you a per hour wage for any time you spend on the Powers of Attorney and then I want to negotiate a fair wage for settling my estate as my executor."

"I would be glad to help, but don't you have family to help you?"

"I'm ninety-eight and have no living family except distant cousins who have nothing to do with me. Sally spoke highly of you and the friendship you shared with her. She trusted you so much, so I want to put my trust in you as well. I'm going to the lawyer today; can I list your name?"

"Yes, as long as you will fill out an end-of-life document I will give you. It covers all the information I will need to be able to process your estate effectively. When we get together to discuss that, we can also talk about my wage."

"I would enjoy that. Do you have time tomorrow afternoon?"

"I do! I love organized people. What about one o'clock?"

"Perfect! I live at sixty-five Mecklenberg Street. See you tomorrow."

After ending the call, she called a taxi and asked that the driver come to her front door to assist her to the car. She then opened the inside door, leaving the storm door closed to keep the weather out. She had everything ready, so she sat by the window with her purse resting in her lap. She held it in the 'death 'grip' that women of her generation used on their purses. While she waited, she reviewed the list of things she needed to accomplish that day.

The taxi arrived, and she saw that Rupert, a sixty-something burly man with a thick mass of curly white hair, was her driver. They were on a first-name basis as he had driven her many times in the past. He always came to the door to help her to the car; she liked that in a man. He saw her in the window and waved. She waved, stood, teetered a bit, but stabilized herself by the time he rang the bell. She raised her voice, so he would hear, "Come in." The screech of hinges long deprived of lubricant told her he was in. He appeared in the living room doorway as she reached for her coat occupying the back of Benny's chair. The January air seemed extra chilly this morning.

"Good morning Alice. Here, let me help you with that." He took the coat and held it as she slid into it comfortably.

"Thank you, Rupert." She noted that there seemed to be so much more material than there was just weeks ago when she wore it to get the last of her medical tests done.

"I'm going to my doctor's appointment; Dr. Phillips in the St. Joseph's Hospital Clinic."

"Come along and I will take you right there." He crooked his arm and felt her take it with a firm, but gentle grip. "Hang on tight."

He got her settled in the car and had her to her appointment in no time. She paid him and as he was helping her out, she asked, "Are you working all day?"

"Yes, I am, why do you ask?"

"I have a few more appointments and I would love for you to take me. Can I call you directly?"

"He gave her his card, "Call me and I will come to get you. Do you know how long you will be here?"

She focused her glance as she thought and then came out of it, "No, but I don't think I will be long."

He helped her into the office area and turned to leave. "Alice, call me when you're ready."

After checking in with the secretary, the nurse led her to a separate area and took her vitals in preparation for her appointment. She then took a seat in the waiting room but was sitting only a few minutes when she heard her name being called. She was tipsy when she stood, and the nurse went over to her and offered an arm for stability. Alice took it and walked with the nurse to an examining room.

After the door clunked shut, she looked around the room to see what she could occupy her mind with, but the door reopened.

Dr. Phillips entered carrying a folder. "You didn't bring anyone with you?"

"No, whatever you have to say I'm ready to hear. After all, I'm ninety-eight, how much longer could I possibly live?" Her spunky response impressed the doctor.

"Well, when you told me about your symptoms, I wanted to check out a couple of possibilities and I was right on one issue. You have a tumour in your lower bowel that has metastasised into your liver and kidneys."

"The pain is increasing so it must be growing quickly. How much time do I have before I will be bedridden and not be able to do anything for myself?"

"It's hard to say. There are painkillers which can help you manage the pain and I can refer you to an Oncologist for some radiation or chemotherapy which might reduce the tumours...'

She stopped him short, "Thank you for the concern, but I know enough about cancer to know that I'm dying, and no amount of treatment is going to make me a spring chicken again." She smiled her '*sweet-little-old-lady*' smile to ease his mind that she knew what she was talking about. "Has Canada legalized medically assisted death yet? If so, I want to have my life ended before I get to be so incapacitated, I'm messing my pants, out of my mind with drugs, or so exhausted I lay in bed waiting to die. None of those things appeal to me, so what can we arrange? In the meantime, while you're arranging it, painkillers sound like a good idea."

He sat looking at her trying to digest what she requested. When he got his wits about him, he responded in a soft caring voice. "I'm sorry, Alice. The law to legalize medically assisted dying in Canada is still being discussed in Parliament. We're months, if not years away from that becoming legal."

"Certainly not fast enough to help me so I have to die the old-fashioned way."

"I can do something about your pain right now." He got his prescription pad, filled out a sheet, and passed it to her. "I would recommend getting your affairs in order if you haven't done so already. You should also make arrangements for some help around the house, with meals, house cleaning and your personal care. We can recommend a few agencies if you would like."

"I have a housekeeper who comes in twice a week and I will ask her if she can do more days or if she knows anyone who could. These housekeepers seem to have a network of their own. I'm off to appointments at my lawyer to update my will as I expected such a diagnosis."

He hesitated at first, but seeing that she was being very pragmatic, he felt he could share something else. "Do you know about Caring Hearts Hospice?"

"Yes, my cousin died there, and I have visited many a friend who died there as well. It's an exceptional facility with wonderful staff. Every person I have spoken to, who has had the opportunity to connect with Caring Hearts, has nothing but great things to say. If you're asking if I would like to go there, I don't have an answer at this moment, but if I decide to go there, can you set this up for me?"

"Yes, I can. I will make some preliminary contacts, see what I must do to organize it. You have no obligation to say yes right now, but in the future, if you decide you would like to, I'll be ready."

"If I decide not to go to Caring Hearts and want to die at home, I would appreciate any information you could share about an agency that will help me do that as well?"

He admired her thoroughness in addressing her situation. "Ask at the front desk when you leave. They will give you a list of all the agencies which could meet your needs."

"Thank you, Dr. Phillips." She got up and started walking to the door. "I have been coming to you for more than 25 years and I have really enjoyed having you as my doctor. You are a good man."

She got the information at the front desk and asked them to call Rupert.

"He will be here shortly and said you should have a seat. He told me he will come in and help you get out to the car."

Rupert arrived, "So, Alice, where am I taking you next?"

"I have an appointment at Zuqqer Law on Waterloo Street in twenty minutes."

"That's lots of time for me to get you there! Let's go." He put his hand over hers as she held onto his arm and walked her to the car.

*****

Alice was seated in one of the client rooms of Zuqqer Law when a dashing young man in his early forties entered. He reached out and shook Alice's hand. "Mrs. DesRoches, it's nice to meet you, my name is David Hardwell and Robert Zuqqer tells me that you want to get your affairs in order. I have your old documents here in case we need to reference them. I see they were created almost twenty years ago, so I imagine things have changed somewhat."

"Most of the people referred to in those documents are long gone, so I need to get things up to date. I do not have long to live so I would appreciate all haste in getting these completed." She informed him in her pragmatic way.

He didn't flinch and went right to work. "I recommend a will, a Power of Attorney, and a medical Power of Attorney. Is this what you were thinking?"

"If these three replace what you have in that folder, I'm good unless you know of something else that I need to consider."

"These are the standard forms and will cover what you need. I understand you want to leave here today with the forms completed, signed and witnessed, so I took the liberty to fill in the information that you gave Robert over the phone, but there is a bit more we need to get from you. Let's get going." He opened a laptop and had her will document up and ready to go.

She sat by his side as he went line by line through the document asking if what he had captured was what she had wanted and if there was anything else that she needed to add. It was a simple will and took no time at all to complete.

He then went onto the Power of Attorney and the Medical Power of Attorney and completed them with the information she supplied. He then reviewed each with her in the same manner as the will. When the last form was done, he sent them to the printer and excused himself with a simple, "I'll get the documents from the printer. We'll have one more review before I bring in witnesses and have you sign."

He returned as promised and laid the two sets of the three stapled forms in front of Alice. She took a pencil from the holder in the centre of the table and held it like a conductor would hold a baton. Using it to orchestrate her progress, she went line by line through each document visually punctuating the silence with nods of her head or a whispered '*yes*' a number of times as she processed through each document he had given her. When she got to the end of the last page of the last document, she closed it, laid her pencil down and announced, "Perfect!"

David Hardwell requested two secretaries to serve as witnesses and the signing was performed on two copies of each document. The lawyer kept one set to be filed and gave one set to Alice to take home.

She had the secretaries contact Rupert and he arrived in the office to assist her out to the car.

"Where would you like to go this time?" He queried as he helped her into the back seat.

"I would like to go to Brunswick Square."

He drove her there, escorted her into the mall and left. She went to the pharmacy to get her prescriptions filled and then decided to get something to eat. She went to the food court, scanned the options for a meal and decided on fish and chips. She normally wouldn't eat a lot of fried food, but, she rationalized that she didn't have much to lose now. She found a seat and sat eating the chips, one at a time, judiciously dipping each in the glossy ketchup, enjoying the whole slow process of eating her meal.

She thought about the morning. When the doctor told her she had cancer, she wasn't surprised; she had been noticing changes in her body and knew something bad had to be going on. She thought about the will and smiled. She hadn't thought much about who would inherit her things until she had to go for the tests and that got her thinking. Her answer came in a dream and she woke up feeling she knew exactly what she wanted to do.

After lunch, she made her way to her two o'clock appointment with her Financial Advisor, Stephen Wycott. Stephen was Benny's investment person and before he died, he directed the household bills to Stephen's office for payment and set it up so that a sum of money would be deposited automatically into Alice's account for her personal use. How lucky for her not to have to concern herself with any of the mundane financial issues. If she needed more money, she made a call and Stephen arranged it for her. Her needs were not that substantial; she had no mortgage, no car, and no credit cards. She had everything she needed.

When she entered his office, the receptionist, Sylvia, greeted her as if they were old friends. Alice had been coming here for many years and had seen several front-office staff in that time, but Sylvia had been here the longest of any of them. She took Alice into a private room and told her that Stephen would be with her in minutes. At two on the dot, Stephen entered the room with her file. "How are you today Alice?"

"Well Stephen, my doctor told me this morning that I have cancer and I don't have much longer to live."

Stephen's eyes welled up, but he dabbed them and regained his composure. "I'm so sorry to hear this, Alice. Is there anything they can do?"

"No, I haven't been feeling right for a while and I knew something was up. I had tests done a few weeks ago and I got the results today; they confirmed my suspicions. I'm ninety-eight. I can't believe that for one thing, who gets this old? For years now I wake every morning surprised I'm still here. Think about it, the odds aren't in my favour. If you're honest with yourself, I could be dead of natural causes long before the cancer gets me." She smiled as she ended that statement and then a sparkle came to her eyes and she continued. "Stephen, the day we're born, we all start our journey to the end of our life, and I have to say that I have been blessed with a long and wonderful journey. I'm really getting the meaning of the old adage; '*All good things must come to an end*.'."

"You're a wise woman Alice. I will miss our chats. What can I do for you today?"

"I need a complete printout of my investments as they sit today, and I want to update the beneficiaries; some have long passed. I always meant to come in and do that before today, but it slipped my mind. With my pending demise, I have the luxury of putting everything in order, so today's the day."

He leafed through the file he brought in and pulled out a summarized list showing each investment with its associated beneficiary. They reviewed the list and Alice made the updates by crossing out existing names and adding new ones. When she was satisfied, he took the list out to Sylvia and she produced the actual beneficiary forms to be signed. When she brought them in, Stephen reviewed each form with Alice and witnessed her signature.

Alice opened her purse and brought out a piece of paper. "Here is the contact information for Wade Jackson, the man I chose for my Executor and both my Powers of Attorney if you need to contact him. I know he will have copies of my death certificate and he will be doing my final income tax return, so you will need it for that, if nothing else." She then pulled out two envelopes and gave them to him. I have written letters that I want you to give the person named on the envelope to read before you tell them how much the investment is worth."

As he accepted the card and each of the envelopes, he placed them in the file. "I will make sure these are read before we discuss the amount."

"Thank you, Stephen. This may be the last time we meet, so I just want to say that both Benny and I have enjoyed working with you. You and your company have made my life so easy for so many years, I cannot tell you how much I appreciate all that you have done for me."

"Thank you. I, too, have enjoyed doing business with you. If you need me for anything, please do not hesitate to call. Goodbye Alice." He gave her a hug and kissed her cheek trying to stay composed, but he couldn't stop his eyes from betraying his regret.

"Goodbye Stephen." She made her way out to the reception area and asked Sylvia to call Rupert to pick her up and take her home. "Tell him I will be in the same spot where he dropped me off."

She put the receiver down and reported, "He said he will be there in ten minutes."

"Thank you, Sylvia. Goodbye dear." Alice walked away with a feeling that her life was finally in order.

Chapter 6

Matthew walked up to Brock's locker, "Want to hang tonight?"

"What do you want to do?"

"Get away from my parents!"

"This is my night to work out. Would you like to join me?"

Matthew lowered his voice, "I dream about working out with you, so don't tease me, Brock. I could pop a boner right here just thinking about this." He looked around and back when he saw the coast was clear, he shot a look at Brock and winked.

"Get your stuff so we can walk home." As Matthew walked away, Brock thought about Andrew and Gregory saying that they thought Matthew was attracted to him. He couldn't deny it any longer, they were probably right. He also had to admit that he was attracted to Matthew.

As they walked along, they talked about the details for that night. After supper, Matthew would come over to 'the Manor' and he and Brock would work out together in the basement gym.

"Are you going to wear a tight t-shirt tonight?"

"Matthew, the way you talk makes me think you're always horny." Brock teased.

"Only when I'm around you or when I'm alone and thinking about you or at night when I'm dreaming about you. Okay, I admit it, I'm always horny."

I hope I don't cause you too many moments of frustration."

"I handle it okay. I have to be careful though because I used my socks to wipe up afterwards and my mother found them when she was doing the wash. The next thing I know Dad is having a man-to-man talk about the sins of masturbation. Now I use tissues and flush them down the toilet. One time, I got lazy and ended up flushing several days worth at once

WAYNE DOUGLAS HARRISON

and plugged the toilet. I almost panicked as the water crested at the rim. I stood there waiting long, anxiety-filled minutes. When it went down a bit before I plunged, I made a silent vow to flush only a couple of day's worth of tissues at a time."

"Thanks for sharing." Brock said sarcastically as they neared the corner where they parted, "See you around seven."

"Seven it is! Wear tight shorts too and you might get the workout of your life!" He winked before he went on his way.

Brock thought about Matthew as he made his way into 'the Manor'. Matthew had even started haunting his thoughts in bed just before falling asleep. He knew he was smitten and asked himself what he was waiting for.

*****

Supper was done and Brock changed into shorter shorts and a tighter athletic shirt that showed his shoulders and biceps well. He knew that once he pumped them up a bit, they would be in their full glory. He couldn't believe he was getting so much enjoyment out of looking forward to Matthew's reaction.

Matthew arrived a bit early and when Brock opened the door Matthew never looked at Brock's face; his eyes did a never-ending scan from his crotch to stomach, to his shoulders, to his arms, to his chest, to his..... without saying a word, but Brock took in how full Matthew's crotch was getting.

"Is anything popping?" Brock teased and he made an exaggerated scan down to Matthew's crotch and raised an eyebrow. "Come on, let's go work out!"

Matthew waved his hand down in front of Brock's body, "What is this get up supposed to mean? I'm not complaining, mind you? Just so you know, I'll be using images of this workout for my night-time relief for weeks to come. Pun intended."

Brock laughed and brought out information he thought Matthew might like to hear, "Andrew and Gregory went to the theatre and we have no guests so I thought I would tantalise. I want tonight to be special."

They headed down to the basement workout room and talked about what they would do. Matthew looked at Brock and stated, "I want you to assess my physique and recommend exercises that would help me tone up."

Matthew was dressed in his loose shorts and t-shirt and Brock needed to see his chest. "You need to remove your shirt."

Matthew eased the shirt over his head and stood waiting for Brock to tease him about being too skinny. "Go ahead, tell me I'm hopeless."

24

"You look like I did before I started working out, so I would say you could achieve whatever goals you want. What are your goals?"

"I want to be fit. Is that the right answer? If I was being completely truthful, I want my boyfriend, when I get one, to find me desirable."

"Your body is only one part of that. Who you are and what you stand for is the bigger part and you don't need any work in those areas."

"Are you saying you find me desirable?"

"I am. You're a very attractive package. Yes, you could tone up some muscles, but tone them for you and let the rest look after itself."

"Thanks, you're so sweet to me. What exercises should I concentrate to build my arms, shoulders and chest?"

"Come over here to the wall chart. This has all of the exercises you'll need, and we can review them."

Matthew stood in front of the chart and Brock started detailing what Matthew would need to focus on to tone the areas he wanted to develop. As he talked, Brock was using his hands to show the muscles on Matthew's body. The more he handled Matthew, the more Matthew's body reacted. As Brock massaged his chest muscles Matthew was very aware that he was tenting his shorts and almost swooned at Brock's touch. Matthew looked at Brock and locked onto his eyes. Brock felt the electricity, leaned in and kissed his lips.

Matthew began to return his pressure but soon pulled back, "I haven't kissed anyone before. I really don't know what to do."

Brock reassured him, "You're doing fine. I have wanted to do this for a while. Relax."

"Brock, I have dreamed of this but never thought you would want me."

"You have told me almost every day since I came out to you that you were interested. Well, I should have told you that I'm interested too." Brock felt something against his leg, reached down and wrapped his hand around Matthew's tent. "What do we have here?"

"OMG Brock, I'm about to explode!"

"Well then, let's not waste this moment." Brock knelt in front and lowered Matthew's shorts. His hands explored Matthew's chest and stomach while his warm mouth planted a series of kisses downward from his mid-abdomen. As he did, Matthew began to vibrate so he moved one of his hands down to Matthew's balls and did light touches with his fingertips until Matthew moaned, "Oh Brock!" When Brock took the tip into his mouth, it was too much for Matthew and he unleashed his pent-up desire. Brock took it deeper into his throat to ride the crest of the wave until it subsided, and he held Matthew there until the vibrating subsided. He stood up and kissed Matthew on the lips again as he pulled his athletic shirt up and over his head to give Matthew free access to his chest.

As Matthew savoured the sensations of the kisses, he realized this was his chance to live his fantasy and began a slow exploration of Brock's body. He propelled his fingertips in slow searching circles over Brock's arms, shoulders, and chest. He luxuriated in the hot smoothness and zeroed in on his nipples as hard as pencil erasers. He tweaked them with light touches and his lips kissed a path down Brock's neck, onto his shoulder and downward to the nipple to lightly suck it between his lips. Brock's moans told him he was right where he needed to be. His hands played over Brock's back and Matthew overloaded his senses comparing this reality to his vivid memories of what he thought this would feel like. He pressed harder and felt Brock's excitement tent his shorts. He used his lips to keep the nipples in play while he moved his hands down to his waist and slid the tight shorts over Brock's smooth hips to begin their descent to the floor. He stood and relished the idea that nothing inhibited the hot flesh connection. Staring Brock in the eyes he reached down and encircled his hand around Brock's excitement. Matthew's grip elicited a moan, and he took his time making the most of the opportunity he had only dreamed of before tonight. As the moans increased in intensity, Matthew slid to his knees keeping a firm grip with one hand and played with the testicles with the other. He took Brock into his mouth and tried to imitate what Brock had done. With gentle touching of the ball sack and creative throat-work, Brock trembled into an explosive ecstasy. When he knew Brock had crested and was coming down, Matthew stood and pressed himself into Brock. He looked him in the eyes and gave him a slow full kiss.

"Brock, you don't know how long I have been waiting for this. Thank you!"

Brock scanned Matthew's face and then recognized his trademark enthusiasm etched in his features. A wave of emotions washed over him. He found himself endeared to Matthew more than ever. Something had changed and Brock kissed him in response, "I'm hoping we'll have many more opportunities, Matthew; will you be my boyfriend?"

Matthew's face blossomed and he erupted, "Yes, yes, yes; I can't think of anything I've wanted more. I need a condition though. We cannot tell anyone about us until I come out to my parents. That could be a long time. Are you okay with that?"

"At one point you said you would never tell them. Let's agree that if we decide to tell someone, we both have to agree."

Matthew thought about it and responded, "Yes, I'm on board. I like that we both have to agree."

Brock continued, "I can promise you anything you need as long as you're in my life. I don't know if you realize how special you are to me."

"You'll just have to show me!" Matthew winked. "If I have you in my life to support me, coming out to my parents doesn't seem as scary. OMG, we now have a special date! January 12th is the date we became a couple. I like the sound of that! I never told you, but I never expected to have a boyfriend until I was out of this city. And I never expected to land you, although I wanted to since the first time I saw you."

Brock blushed, "I never thought I would ever be free enough to have a boyfriend. Of course, I was in such a quandary about my sexual orientation, I didn't have any hopes for a relationship. Everything is happening so fast."

They dressed and hit the machines. The workout was good but ended up being secondary to the emotions each was feeling.

When they finished, they went up to the living room. Matthew closed all the drapes. "I want us to be free to be a couple, so I don't want anyone looking in."

Matthew sat on the sofa and patted the space next to him. Brock joined him and they sat there experiencing the newness. Brock leaned back and Matthew nestled into him.

Brock wanted to have Matthew talk about their new secret; he needed to know what the boundaries really were. "Andrew and Gregory will be home soon, how do you feel about telling them? They have been nothing but supportive of me."

"I guess I would be good with them knowing. I do want to make sure we keep it between the four of us. Okay?"

"Well, there are a few more people we can trust."

"Who?"

"What about Mackenzie?" Brock looked into Matthew's eyes and waited.

"We know she will be okay, yes we can tell her; who else?"

"Mammie. When we put up her tree at Christmas, she told me she thought we were boyfriends. I told her we weren't but that I was interested. She made me promise that if we became boyfriends, I would tell her. How do you feel about that?"

"She was alright with you being gay and having a boyfriend?"

"Yes, she talked about it as if it happened everyday. She doesn't have a bigoted bone in her body."

"She accepted you and your own parents didn't, that is just fucked up."

"Yes, it is fucked up. Mammie was wonderful. It gave me hope my parents would accept me but we both know how that turned out."

"Okay but I want us to tell her together, as a couple. There is no one else, is there? Think hard."

"No, there isn't another living soul."

Just then, they heard footsteps ascending the verandah stairs and a key in the lock. The door opened and as the guys entered, they were chatting about the theatre, oblivious to anything else. Gregory hung up their coats as Andrew continued talking. They turned away from the closet and startled themselves when they saw Brock and Matthew. They did a double take when they saw how close they were. Andrew summed it up, "Well, did you two finally have that talk?"

Matthew couldn't contain his enthusiasm, "We did more that talk! We are boyfriends!"

Gregory added, "We have to say, we are not surprised that it happened, only that it took you both so long. Congratulations!"

Matthew was excited, "Apart from the two of you, we are only telling Mackenzie and Mammie."

Gregory continued, "We will keep your secret. I am glad you told us who else will know. That makes it so easy for us!"

Chapter 7

Mackenzie walked into the kitchen and found her mom sitting at the table, looking out the window into the raging snowstorm. It had caused cancellations across the city, including all schools and the university. She noticed the dark circles under her mother's puffy, red eyes, evidence of her recent crying. "Mom, are you getting any sleep?"

"A little, but I worry about Brock and how he is doing. I miss his cheery personality and our wonderful talks. I hate that this has happened." Martha was being upfront which was rare, but that told Mackenzie that her father wasn't home.

"Did Dad go to work?"

"Yes, they are working inside today, so he felt he could get a lot done by going in."

"Mom, you say you hate that you kicked Brock out. You recognize that you do have some blame in that, don't you?"

"Your father kicked him out, not me."

"You supported it and didn't say anything to stop it. I blame you both equally. When Dad said Brock was dead to him and not welcome in the family, you just stood there without protesting. He killed off your child and you stood silently back and watched as your son walked out of the only home he has ever known. What kind of a parent does that?" Mackenzie was flushed in the face as all the injustice of that evening came rushing back.

Martha's shame was overwhelming. She started sobbing and buried her face in her hands.

Mackenzie's heart wouldn't let her be too mad at her mother in her condition. She knew things were exactly where they needed to be to get her mom on the road to healing. "I have something that can help you resolve this, that is, if you really want to have Brock back in your life."

"Of course I want him back in my life, but I don't know about your father. He can be so proud." Martha sighed.

"Proud? Proud of what? Oh, yes, he disowned his only son and kicked him out of the house because of his ignorant, red-necked beliefs. Now that's really something to make him proud. Mom, you don't come off any better you know and you disappointed Brock so much. Dad's reaction wasn't a surprise, but yours was."

"Don't say that, I'm not like your father." She broke down. Mackenzie put a box of tissues on the table in front of her, she took several and blew her nose. "How can I ever fix this mess?"

Mackenzie caught her Mother's eye. "I told you I had something that would help you get Brock in your life, but you ignored me like I didn't even say it. So, do you want some help getting Brock back?"

Martha was puzzled at her daughter's statement. "What kind of help?"

Mackenzie explained about the monthly Pflag support meetings, who attends, and how they worked. "You participate to your comfort level and learn from others in the room about LGBT issues. I have gone with Brock to the fall meetings, and before that, I have supported other people who are gay."

"What if people see me going in?" Martha shuddered in panic.

"Really Mom, you care more about what other people think than having your son back in your life? Did you ever think of what they would think of you and Dad if they learned you kicked your son out of his home? I encourage you to mention this at work to your coworkers who are gay there and see what they think. Your behaviours are coming out of your ignorance about gay people. I say ignorance meaning your lack of knowledge. Pflag is a chance to educate yourself about who your son is. He can't change who he is, he was born gay, but you have a chance to change who you are through educating yourself. The meeting is this Friday evening, and we are going. Be ready at six-thirty."

*****

Mackenzie drove her mother to the meeting and parked the car in the parking lot. It took her ten minutes to talk her mother out of the car. Finally, she opened Martha's door, "Come on Mom; nobody will see you."

Martha put one foot out onto the ground, but before the second was placed outside, she put up the voluminous hood on her coat and put on a pair of sunglasses even though it was already dark. Mackenzie saw the irony in her mom's ill-conceived disguise. Anyone who knew Martha, knew her car.

Martha hunched over so no one could see any of her face as she followed Mackenzie into the building. Mackenzie encouraged her mother out of her coat and glasses and when Martha turned around, Andrew was approaching. "Welcome back Mackenzie and welcome Martha, it's nice to meet again. I'm Andrew Wallace and we first met a few years back at a university function that was held at Mahogany Manor. I am glad you're here. I'm hoping Pflag will provide you with some comfort."

Martha was so nervous, but she tried to pretend she wasn't. "Thank you. Mackenzie suggested I come but I'm not sure I should be here."

Andrew looked at Martha with compassion for her uncertainty and responded, "Your son is living with us because he isn't welcome in your home. I don't say that to hurt you, but more to make the point that your family needs Pflag now more than ever. You are in the right place to start healing."

Martha stared at him, turned and walked over to a window where she stood looking out into nothing until Mackenzie went over to her. "Mom, we need to go in now; the meeting will be starting soon." Martha followed her into the room and selected a seat close to the door. Mackenzie wondered if this was intentional but left it alone.

The meeting got underway and in no time the introductions were progressing around the table. When it got to Martha she simply said, "My name is Martha" and went silent.

Mackenzie went next, "I'm here to support my mom." Reaching out and taking Martha's hand. "My brother came out to the family last week and we're here to learn how to go forward as a family."

The meeting got through the introductions and into the topic areas. One of the topics being explored came from a parent who was having a difficult time with their daughter being gay and the conversation was insightful and robust. Mackenzie was pleased with the topic and thought her mother would join in the discussion. Martha sat listening and didn't participate.

Mackenzie decided to risk upsetting her mother and joined in, "I understand it's hard on some parents, but what about the other family members? My brother is not allowed in our home and I have been forbidden to mention his name. I think we need to understand the full impact on everyone involved, the gay child, the parents, the siblings and the extended family members."

Martha turned to Mackenzie, narrowed the focus of her eyes, and glared at her without saying anything; well, at least nothing verbally.

Mackenzie's lead got the discussion to focus on the whole family and most of the participants shared something about their family. She was pleased with herself that things were being said by others that zeroed in on what the Mathesons were going through; thoughts, feelings, hopes, and fears. Some of the parents offered the titles of books they found helpful. She hoped her mother was taking this all in but she couldn't tell. She opened her backpack and brought out the book that had stayed in isolation on the dining room table as if touching it would cause some strange fatal disease. "This is a book that my brother gave to my parents the night he came out. It has great reviews and people are saying it's very helpful, but no one in our home would know because it hasn't been opened yet. I stress the 'yet' because I'm making a commitment to help Mom read it. She hasn't said much tonight, but she wants Brock back in her life and coming to these Pflag meetings is the first step that we'll continue in the coming months. Reading this book will be step two. I will share our progress in future meetings." Mackenzie knew her mom could be manipulated, and she hoped this public manipulation strategy would pay off in spades. She also knew she was treading on thin ice. She counted on her mother being sincere in fixing this 'issue' as she referred to it. Mackenzie was certain that when things started to derail for her mother, she would use the '*wanting Brock back in her life*' card and that would bring her mother back on course.

The meeting ended with Martha not having said anything beyond her introduction. Mackenzie was almost certain she would get a terse reprimand for what she shared at the meeting, but when they got in the car, Martha started to discuss the meeting. She reviewed what was said and how she felt about the topic, making correlations to their situation. She asked for advice about her own behaviours, and what she needed to do to fix them.

Mackenzie was delighted and asked her mother if she would read the book Brock gave them.

"Tonight, I had an '*aha*' moment. That was when, I believe Tyler, said '*the path out of ignorance is education.*' and I couldn't have agreed more. I thought about my ignorance, and it's difficult for me to say I'm ignorant, but I am, and I need to educate myself. I guess I wasn't ready to hear I was ignorant when you told me earlier this week, but I was ready tonight. When you brought that book out of your backpack, I was ashamed that I hadn't read it. I admonish my students on a regular basis for ignoring the information they readily have available to them in their textbooks or online. I drew a parallel to my ignoring a great resource right in front of me. Yes, I will read it."

Mackenzie was amazed at what she had just heard and thought she would use it to gain more. "As you learn, do you think you could start sharing with Dad? You have a way of getting him to listen and he needs to address his ignorance as well."

Martha thought about it and responded, "My goal is to get my family back together. That can't happen if your father doesn't get educated too. I'll do what I can to help him grow, but I need to grow first because he is a formidable foe to try to educate. I need to have all my facts in place first."

Chapter 8

Mackenzie parked in their driveway and Martha, hand on the door handle, simply sat there without making any motions to get out. Mackenzie saw something percolating and decided to sit in silence to let her mom have the time she needed. Something clicked in her mom and she spoke. "So, my next step should be reading Brock's book." She lifted the book and looked at it as if it was written in a language other than English.

Mackenzie wondered what was happening. "What's wrong Mom? You don't seem sure of yourself."

Martha looked at her and started to cry, "It can't be as simple as reading this book, can it? I'm beating myself up for not reading it that awful night. I just let it sit on the table for a week and I could have been reading it. I guess I'm afraid that the answer is so simple that it will tell me I'm a terrible mother. When Brock stood in front of me that night trying to get his message across, he asked, '*where is my mother?*' and in that moment, I knew I had failed my child. I don't believe there is a worse feeling a mother could have." She wiped her eyes and blew her nose.

As much as Mackenzie wanted to be mad, her heart melted for her mother, "Mom, you're beginning a journey of discovering who your son is. We live in a world where people like Brock feel they must pretend to be someone they aren't, if they are to be accepted. You never entertained the thought that you had a gay child; that was always someone else's problem. It is only a problem if you make it one. You won't help yourself by looking back because you cannot change anything that has already passed. No amount of guilt, shame, regret, or time spent on 'should've, would've, could've' is going to help fix this family; education is our only way. Reading this book is a good place to start. I would love to have discussions with you about what you read so we both can learn."

33

"You already accept Brock being gay; what more do you need to learn? Me, I have to start at ground zero." Martha seemed defeated.

"I accept Brock because I do not see gay as anything bad, or shameful. It isn't a problem for me. It's just another attribute of the brother I dearly love. I believe you're having a hard time because somewhere in your development you were told that being gay was, in some way, bad and you swallowed it hook, line, and sinker. I have a good understanding of gay, but I don't know everything. I would welcome learning more so I can help more ignorant people. I'm fed up with elite-thinking people who feel anyone who is different is fair game for shunning or abuse."

"How did I get a daughter so wise?"

"You taught me the value of continuous education. Now it's your turn to educate yourself."

Martha perked up and smiled at Mackenzie. "Thank you for encouraging me; I need it. I'm going to start reading this book tonight." Martha opened the door, got out as a gust of freezing air filled the car. "Are you still going to Jill's place?"

"Yes, I expect to be home by eleven or a little after."

Mackenzie backed out of the driveway as Martha went into the house.

Martha hung her coat up and walked toward the kitchen, passing the living room on her way. She saw Grant watching TV and stopped at the archway, "How was your evening?"

He was enthralled in his show as she knew he would be and responded with one word, "Good." and kept his eyes glued to the TV.

She went to the kitchen and boiled some water for tea. She went to the door and asked Grant if he wanted anything, but again, he was engrossed in his show and barely responded. "No thanks."

She made her cup of tea, sat at the kitchen table. Started reading Brock's book accompanied by a pad of paper, a pen, and a highlighter. She wrote copious notes and questions for her discussion with Mackenzie. She had just finished writing a note when Grant walked in.

Grant saw her set up at the table like so many times before and knew she was focused. "Where were you tonight?"

Martha didn't see this going well, but decided if she wanted to fix this family, the truth was the best answer. "Mackenzie and I went to a Pflag meeting."

"What is a Pflag meeting?" Grant inquired.

Martha hesitated and thought '*Here goes*' and let it out into the room. "Pflag is a support meeting for parents, friends, and family members of lesbians and gays. I'm hoping you will attend future meetings with me."

Grant's ego feathers ruffled, "Why the hell would you go to that meeting? And where is your head that you would think I would go to one of those faggot meetings?"

34

Martha stood her ground but didn't raise her voice to the level he had used. "To learn about gay issues from others going through a difficulty like we are."

"Difficulty! What specific difficulty are we going through that a meeting like that would help?"

Martha had known his response would be something like that and, even so, she was disappointed. "Oh, Grant, our family is torn apart because of our attitudes. Being gay isn't a choice. We have a gay son...."

Grant stood tall and spoke with authority. "Don't feed me that brainwashed bullshit you were fed at that meeting. Brock isn't gay, he just needs a kick in the arse. Trust me, stay the course we have laid out and he'll forget all about being gay. What are you reading, more propaganda? You know all you need to know about gay issues; gay is disgusting. Brock is simply confused and needs to suffer a little to help him make better choices. You wait, when Brock sees we're not going to back down, he will choose not to be gay and we will welcome him back into our family and our home."

"Grant, I think you are wrong." Martha looked at him to see how he took that, and she saw that it wasn't good, so, she decided, '*Why stop now?*' and continued. "At the meeting, a young man said the cure for ignorance is education and I'm educating myself. Brock gave us this book the night you kicked him out. I'm going to read every word and learn what I need to learn so I can have my son back in my life."

Grant was livid. "How dare you say I'm wrong?"

"I didn't say you were wrong; I said I think you're wrong." She looked at him and held his glare. "From what I learned in tonight's meeting, being gay isn't a choice. Brock told us that when he came out to us, but we didn't listen to him or give him any credit for knowing what he was talking about. We shut him down without any facts to back up what we believed. He has been researching being gay and understands it a whole lot better than either you or me, but we kicked him out of our lives because of our ignorance." She paused there to give him time to think, especially about the last two words.

Grant stormed over to Martha, but she was determined not to flinch. She stood her ground even when he stuck his face in front of hers. "So, you seem to have bought into this Pflag garbage." He shook his head in disbelief, "Are you really calling me ignorant?"

It took all of Martha's resolve to not fall into her typical behaviours and back down. She kept her face in position just inches from his. "I too, had some difficulty with being ignorant so I googled a definition, and it means: '*Lacking knowledge, information, or awareness about something in particular.*' With that in mind, we're both lacking knowledge, information and awareness about what gay is and what it means. Therefore, to answer your question, I don't just believe we are ignorant, I know we are. The sooner we become educated, the sooner our family will be back together."

"I'm not standing here listening to this god-damned foolishness." Grant was so enraged that his spittle sprayed Martha's face. "You do what you want, but don't expect me to be part of it!" He turned and stormed out of the kitchen.

As Grant left, she used the back of her sleeve to wipe her face and thought about getting the family back together. She raised her left eyebrow and in a low voice, to no one in particular, she said, "So, that's how it's going to be. Mark my words, I may have lost this battle, but I will be damned if I'm going to lose this war." She knew there would be challenges, but now, by standing her ground, she had a better understanding of how difficult this was going to be. This war was going to call for strategies and tactics she never used before, but then again, she never had to fight for anything this important.

Chapter 9

Over the past week, Alice had been reflecting on Brock and Matthew's visit where they announced they were boyfriends. When she thought about them sitting in the living room, she remembered the positive vibes they gave off. She got such a good feeling out of seeing them together. The best part was that Brock was smiling again.

She sensed it was the right time to share her news. He had called earlier in the day and asked if he could visit. They agreed on seven that evening. "Oh Honey, that would be perfect. I have something I want to share with you."

As Brock walked to her house, he noticed that, all of a sudden, large fluffy flakes were fluttering all around him. Not enough to have it accumulate more than a dusting, but he was emersed in the silence as they made their way to the ground. They seemed to work their magic on his anxiety of being so close to his parents' home. It still gave him a funny feeling not to be able to think about it as his home, but he was starting to get used to it.

As he approached, he saw Mammie standing in the window. He waved and she waved back. He perceived that something was different in the wave; it didn't carry the same energy that she employed at other times. He determined that she must be tired.

She greeted him at the door with a hug and he noted she seemed frailer than just a week ago. "Take your coat off and have a seat. I have mugs of hot chocolate waiting for us."

They sat on the couch, angled so they faced each other with their knees almost touching. She had planned this so they could easily see each other as they talked. She asked how life was at '*the Manor*' and about school. He noticed that she didn't explore the answers he gave like she normally would, simply accepting them before moving on. It was all too perfunctory.

Brock became leery. Something was up. He needed to know before his imagination took over. "Mammie, I have been curious about what you wanted to share with me ever since you told me."

"Honey, I have been blessed with a wonderful long life and when I go to bed at night I wonder if I will wake in the morning to live another day. I'm not paranoid; more realistic I would say knowing that we all have to go sometime. Anyway, I would like to know if I can put you as my next of kin on my Medicare card. If something happens, you would be the first person they would call."

"I would be honoured. I was scared you were going to tell me you were ill." He cringed as he said it because it brought back the thought of her frailness.

"Well, Honey, that is another thing I want to talk to you about. I am ill, but I don't want you to be scared. I haven't been feeling right over the past number of months. When I started having pain, I went to my doctor who ordered tests in mid-December. I got the results a couple of weeks ago. I have terminal cancer." She was watching his reaction to what she was saying. His facial muscles hardened as he tried to maintain control, but his eyes betrayed him. They welled up, his lip quivered, and when he replayed the words '*terminal cancer*' he broke down.

Tears flowed freely; he couldn't stop them. He wrapped his massive arms around her frail body. Through his emotion, he was able to choke out, "I don't want to lose you."

"Honey, you will have me in your heart for the rest of your life. I know I have a place there."

He was at a loss for words. What do you say to someone you love when they tell you they are dying? "You're a big part of my life. I cannot remember a time when you were not part of it. The love you have shown me is anchored in my heart and there is no possible way that I could ever forget you." He paused to clear his head. He knew cancer could be very painful and needed to know, "Are you in much pain?"

"Some pain, but the doctor gave me pills that seem to manage it, for now anyway. I found I couldn't cope with everything around the house so, instead of moving into a nursing home, I increased Paula's hours and hired her friend, Valerie. They work well together and manage it all themselves, so all the days are covered. They are here from nine in the morning until nine in the evening. Valerie is a sweet woman, and she was here today. I asked her to leave early tonight so I could have you to myself. Both ladies are a godsend helping me with all the housework, grocery shopping, meals, and my personal care. I'm finding even the simplest task to sometimes be too much. I am now coming to understand the saying '*Getting old isn't for sissies.*' where I never connected to it before."

He smiled at her humour. "It sounds like you have thought of everything. Promise me that if there is anything I can do; you won't hesitate to let me know."

"One thing I miss is seeing you every day since you moved. My days are numbered. You brighten even the gloomiest ones for me, so I would love to see you more often. Could you fit me in? Knowing I have limited time makes me feel I can be a little selfish."

"I promise I will! I need you to be honest with me and tell me everything with no holding back. I want no surprises. I hope you don't mind me asking questions." He paused, a question was eating away at him and he decided he would ask it. "You've known for a while but kept it from me. Why?"

"Oh Honey, I will be honest with you. I suspected I was ill but didn't tell you sooner because I didn't want to ruin your Christmas or birthday. I wanted to wait until my doctor confirmed my suspicions last week. I even hesitated to tell you now, being so close to your parents kicking you out and all, but I felt you needed to know sooner than later."

Brock locked his eyes to hers and asked, "How long do you have?"

"The doctors really can't give me a definite date. The way things are progressing, my doctor expects I might have less than two months. Things are changing so fast; each day brings more pain and less independence. I will know when I need to do something different. I'm not afraid; I have had a good life."

"That means around the end of March." The realization triggered a new wave of tears, but he continued. "Do you plan to die at home, or will you be going to the hospital at some point?"

"I gave that careful consideration. When I find I can't get around here easily or I need to have better pain management, I will go to Caring Hearts Hospice on the West Side. That is, if they have an opening when I'm ready. I've told my doctor of my decision and he is making all the necessary arrangements."

"I have a friend whose grandmother died there. His family found the staff to be wonderful; they take really good care of the patients. I hope there is an opening when you need it."

"If there isn't, I can always go to the palliative care ward at the Regional Hospital. It isn't my first choice, as I want a less clinical environment, but I have heard good things about it too."

"I will be here for you no matter where you go."

Chapter 10

Mackenzie dropped into '*the Manor*' with some mail that had arrived for Brock. Gregory invited her to stay for lunch. When she entered the kitchen, she saw that everyone was seated and ready to eat. "Boy, did I choose a great time to visit!"

After getting hugs all round, she took her seat between Andrew and Gregory and across from Matthew who, she knew, would never consider relinquishing his seat next to Brock.

Matthew had become an almost permanent fixture at '*the Manor*' since he and Brock became a '*couple*', a word he used to punctuate almost every one of his statements. Today was no exception when he said, "Now that we are a couple, these are our designated seats at this table."

Mackenzie took him to task, "Matthew, you need to give it a rest."

He refuted her dig, "How can I get the mileage out of having my hunky boyfriend if I can't tell anyone but you people. So, my advice is, get used to '*couple*' because I worked hard for this and I'm not giving it up easily!"

Brock turned to look at Matthew, "So, you worked hard, did you?"

"It is hard work being this charming all the time, but it was worth it." At which he put one arm around Brock like he was the prize.

Mackenzie broke in with, "Gag me with a spoon!" as she picked one up and acted out putting it down her throat. Looking toward Andrew and Gregory, "On a serious note, your big Valentine's event is coming up and we are all booked to work it. Any details we should know?"

Andrew tapped a book sitting on the table next to his place. "I have just finalized all the plans with the client. This is a big one and it will be formal. They brought a designer in a week ago to take measurements for the decorations and they will be showing up around noon that day. They expect to take about 4 hours to install the decorations. I can hardly wait to see how the place looks with what they plan to do." He then looked in his book, "They have chosen a wonderful assortment of food for 75 people. No one should leave here hungry. They have also booked all the guest rooms so they will have the place all to themselves and their guests."

Mackenzie thought about the size and asked, "So this is a formal event. What do we wear, our normal serving clothes?"

"Good question, he did request something special!" He looked at his notes again, "They have requested that all staff wear black pants, black socks and shoes, white shirt, black cummerbund, and black bow ties. We have the shirts, bow ties, and cummerbunds and we expect you each have your own pants, shoes, and socks. Mackenzie, we have a men's small shirt that I think will fit you okay, but it would be good for you to try it on, just in case."

Brock was listening to all of the details and sized it up, "They seem to be sparing no expense. Are they Valentine's Day nuts or what is the real reason for this grand show?"

Andrew pondered his question. "I guess I never gave it any thought except to get everything right. The couple is meticulous in their planning, so I want everything to meet their expectations. The event takes place on Saturday the thirteenth and they did stress that Valentine's Day is on Sunday so a big reveal of some sort will happen after midnight. They expect guests to start departing around one o'clock."

"I love surprises!" exclaimed Mackenzie.

"So do I!" said an excited Matthew.

Andrew surveyed the faces, "This event happens this coming Saturday, so I expect everyone to be here Friday to go over the planning and determine what we all need to be on board. Let's do supper Friday evening and we will make it a joint planning session. It should only take a couple of hours. Is that good for everyone?"

All heads nodded.

"Great, see you for supper at five-thirty on Friday."

*****

'The Manor' was a beehive of activity getting ready for the Valentine's party. Brock, Matthew, Andrew, Gregory and Mackenzie were following the lists they developed the previous evening at their joint planning session. Attention was being paid to the special touches the client had requested.

The designer brought four staff who were working their magic and the place was transforming into a true place of romance. Lush garlands of greenery festooned with red sweetheart roses, baby's breath, and sparkling rice lights swirled down the pillars in the living room and dining room and cascaded down the banisters. Two gigantic, overlapping, hearts of red roses formed a backdrop to a decorated pergola in the turret area of the entry hall which created a photo opportunity for guests attending the party. Runner-like centre pieces with long-stem red roses found their place on the top of the piano, down the centre of the dining table, the reception desk, and on the fireplace mantle. Copious rose arrangements populated tabletops and ledges throughout. Everyone agreed the mood for romance the clients had wanted was more than met by the time the decorating crew had packed up and left.

Late afternoon brought the hum of preparations to an end. The building was quiet. Brock and Matthew were finishing in the kitchen and announced they were going to take a well-deserved break. "We've overheard the wonderful comments about the decorations, but we haven't had a chance to see them since they were completed. Let's go and experience it for ourselves before the party starts."

"Wait here a few more minutes while we go out and turn the accent lighting on. You need to experience the full effect." Gregory said as he followed Andrew out of the kitchen.

Andrew poked his head around the doorframe and announced, "Now is your chance." In the butler's pantry, Andrew covered Brock's eyes while Gregory covered Matthew's eyes and they led them into the dining room. They positioned them facing each other so they would see different views of the room and explained, "OK, on the count of three, we will uncover your eyes; one, two, three."

Brock was looking toward the windows and saw Matthew's expression change into one of wonder. He had to see what caused the change and turned around to see things from Matthew's vantage point. They were staring at the staircase framed by the decorated pillars of the dining room archway. The sight was awe-inspiring. They did a slow complete rotation, so they could digest the whole mood.

Brock spoke first, "I can't find words to describe what I'm seeing and feeling. The designers certainly delivered on their '*a night of romance*' theme."

Matthew was quiet with wide and shining eyes. Looking at Brock, he finally spoke, "I know what feeling." He stepped forward and kissed him.

Gregory saw the kiss and interrupted, "Whoa Matthew, don't get too deep into the mood, we have a party to work."

They all laughed, and Matthew added, "This romance mood works for me. The way I see it is, romance is the hope for sex, is it not? Therefore, romance must be another more socially acceptable word for horny because you hear romance all the time but very seldom do we hear horny. Whether it is or not, it makes me horny!"

"You must have about ten minutes left on your break; good luck. After that, you are on our time and we don't pay for that kind of a break. See you in the kitchen in ten." Andrew winked, as he followed Gregory and left Brock and Matthew standing in the dining room.

Matthew looked at Brock and raised an eyebrow, "Ten minutes is better than none."

Brock shook his head and responded, "Maybe on your own. Why don't you use the ten minutes to take a cold shower?" He smirked and gave a soft punch to Matthew's arm.

Chapter 11

Around seven o'clock, a polished gay couple in their thirties arrived dressed in tuxes. Andrew greeted them and, after they had checked their list with his, he showed them around. They stood in the archway between the living room and dining room and took in the panoramic view. Everywhere they looked were twinkling lights, a sea of red roses, greenery, and baby's breath, and they noted details they had forgotten but were thrilled that they added to the overall effect. The doorbell rang and the guests they had chosen to stay in the B&B rooms were arriving. While being greeted by the couple, the guests oohed and awed as they looked around. They congratulated the couple on their taste before heading up to their rooms to get changed for the party.

The clients oversaw the laying out of the food and nodded their approval while they checked things off their list attached to a clip board. It appeared that Andrew wasn't put off by their behaviour. In fact, he had expected it even though he had never worked with someone who needed to be in so much control. Earlier, one of the more positive things he said to the others was that this couple knew exactly what they wanted. He hoped he was able to interpret their needs and deliver to their expectation.

Gregory, who was taking the lead on the food preparation, joined Andrew and watched the couple. They saw the items being checked off and they waited.

Matthew marched into the kitchen with a red face and confronted Mackenzie and Brock, "Do you guys feel like we are being scrutinized by that couple? I don't know if I can handle it!"

"Wow, Matthew, what got you so upset? When I spoke with Andrew about tonight, he expected the couple to do exactly what they are doing. They are only interested in everything being perfect. It is not about us as much as it is about the event meeting their expectations." Mackenzie tried to assure him.

"I can't believe Andrew and Gregory have to watch that couple rate them so blatantly. How must they feel? I had thought it would be wonderful serving this event for a gay couple. I was looking forward to it but when they started their '*quality-control checking*', I half expected them to bring out a stopwatch, and time everything. Who do they think they are in their expensive tuxes and carrying on with such authority?" Matthew's face had flushed as he spoke and ended with a furrowed brow.

Observing Matthew's judgemental distress, Brock took his hand and led him into the back hall for a private talk. "Matthew, tonight, is a very important night for that couple. Yes, they are over-the-top, but that is the way they are making sure everything is right."

"They make me nervous. I guess it is more than nervous, they make me angry. I go out there and I'm afraid I'll drop something." Matthew said as he frowned and lowered his head.

Brock put his bent index finger under Matthew's chin and tilted his head up so he could look him in the eyes. "You're doing a great job. You always do! Remember, you wouldn't be working this event if Andrew and Gregory didn't have faith in you. Chill a little and just keep doing what you're doing," He leaned in and gave him a kiss.

Matthew looked at Brock and his heart melted, "Oh, alright but they are spooking me. I'll try my best to not let them get to me." He followed Brock into the kitchen, and picked up a tray, "Here goes! I'm going to be faking it completely." He replaced his solemn look with a bright smile and walked out of the kitchen.

The couple went over to Andrew and Gregory and shook their hands. Robert, the main contact, spoke, "This is exactly like we pictured the event to be. Thank you for the amazing job you've done for us! I'm looking forward to seeing everyone's reactions!"

Calvin, Robert's partner, added, "This is a special night for us and your attention to detail has surpassed anything we have contracted before. Thank you."

Gregory spoke, "It is always good to work with people who know what they want."

Andrew broke in, "It is almost eight and we expect you will be greeting your guests soon. Would you like to take a breather before the onslaught?"

Calvin confessed, "I need to pee before I get too busy. Can you show us to our room?"

"Follow me." Andrew led them to the room on the main floor.

When they re-emerged before eight, they did a slow walk-through to capture the mood and were all smiles. They were thrilled with what had been done and called the transformation perfect for their '*evening of romance*' theme. Shortly after, a selection of guests from the B&B rooms came down and were shown around by the couple who wanted to do all the people-hosting for the night.

Joe, the bartender was ready and waiting and Brock, Mackenzie, and Matthew were doing last-minute checks on everything.

Guests, classically dressed in their finest evening apparel, started arriving and were greeted by their hosts. They had been asked to dress in black and white with a red accessory in honour of Valentine's Day. The result was stunning and enhanced the overall theme. The effect of the decorations, the white linen-covered tables, and all the accent lighting bedazzled the guests while soft jazz set the mood as it danced about the room. The evening was ramping up to be a party to remember.

The clients wanted pictures of every guest so the photographer would encourage each person or couple to have their picture taken under the heart-decorated pergola. Once the posed pictures were completed, the photographer roamed the room taking candid shots.

The evening was executed with the precision of a well-oiled machine and from the emptying platters, the amount of emptied drink glasses that were collected over the evening, the couples dancing, and the overall laughter, the evening was a success.

Matthew had calmed down and seemed to be enjoying the evening. At one point he motioned for Brock to follow him out to the back hall off the kitchen where he exclaimed, "Did you notice the guests tonight?"

"Yes, a very attractive group of people."

"Not just that. There is almost every kind of person or couple out there! Lesbian, gays, transgender, straight, and who knows what else." Matthew said with a bewildered look.

"Yes, there is a lot of diversity in the room. Is something causing you concern?"

"Oh, I'm not concerned, I'm just so pleased. Did you see they are all acting as if it is normal?"

"Maybe the couple created an environment in their lives where this is normal." Brock said as he watched Matthew's face.

"I'm just so thrilled to be part of this. It gives me hope."

Brock hugged Matthew and gave him a soft kiss. "So, you aren't mad at the couple any longer?"

Matthew blushed, "I'm sorry for that outburst. I get it now, but I wasn't getting any part of that earlier."

"I saw that, but I'm glad you're over it now." Brock smiled, "I want us to enjoy this night and maybe, someday, we can create an environment in our life that expands what normal is."

"I hope so." Matthew smiled.

"We'd better get back out there before Mackenzie comes looking for us."

*****

At midnight, Brock turned the music down low so the hosts could do their announcement. Robert spoke first. "Thank you for coming to this special evening. It is officially Valentine's Day and we are fulfilling a fantasy we have had since we met."

Calvin picked up where Robert left off, "We have always wanted to get married on Valentine's Day and in a few minutes, we will be exchanging vows. Thank you for coming to our wedding!"

The crowd's faces showed surprise as they erupted with cheers and words of congratulations.

The couple thanked them and moved over to the pergola where they stood with the hearts behind them. An attractive lady walked out of the crowd to officiate. She wore a red satin vintage 1950s haute couture calf length gown, elbow-length black gloves, black stilettos, and a string of pearls looking like the most elegant officiate anyone had ever seen.

Each of the husbands recited vows they had written and exchanged rings. After the short ceremony guests congratulated the couple one-on-one and had pictures taken with them. As the final guests were having their pictures taken, the excitement had calmed down and they spent time in casual conversation. As soon as one couple got their coats to leave, more and more did the same and, as predicted, most were gone by one o'clock. The guests staying the night gradually filtered up the stairs and the room emptied.

While Brock was attending to requests from the hosts, Matthew walked Mackenzie home at one o'clock.

Matthew had returned to find the guys talking to the couple, so he went to the kitchen where Brock was finishing the cleanup. They had worked together through the event managing the cleanup so only half an hour was needed to finish.

Andrew and Gregory bid good night to the couple as they retired to their room and they went into the kitchen. "Wow, you guys dismantled the food and have the cleanup done; you're amazing! We just finished talking to the newly married couple and they have nothing but great things to say about all that everyone did to make their surprise Valentine's wedding such a success. They are beyond thrilled! Thank you both and of course Mackenzie for your wonderful support. We couldn't have done it without you. Now, if we could set the dining room table for breakfast, we could all call it a night."

After everything was in place, Gregory spoke, "You two had better get up to bed, you have to be bushed! The guests will be down for a ten o'clock breakfast, so make the best use of your time and make sure you get enough rest. See you in the morning!" Andrew waited for Gregory to finish, winked, and shooed them away with both hands.

They went up to Brock's room at the top of the stairs. Tonight, would be Matthew's first overnight stay and he and Brock wanted to make the most of it. Even though they should have been totally exhausted, the excitement of sleeping together for their first full night had their hormones revving. The anticipation brought them together in secret spaces several times during the party for stolen kisses and tender embraces, but they were finally behind closed doors and no one would disturb them.

Brock stood in front of Matthew and whispered, "Happy Valentine's Day!" and gave him a slow kiss. The lightness of their touch sent shivers in all directions. The effect was like many electrified fingers lightly defining pathways across their skin. It was almost too much to bear but proved not enough to stop them as they joyfully succumbed to the sensations.

Locking gazes, their eyes spoke wordlessly of mixed and confusing messages, of a forbidden love that they fought to make honest and real. They struggled to put these new, undefined feelings into context while they experienced love in its simplest of forms.

One by one, buttons were found and released. They each pressed their palms lightly on the other's chest and luxuriated in the heat as they worked the shirts up and over the shoulders causing them to float from their bodies and land cloud-like behind them. Not feeling any rush, they pressed their bodies together, caught each other's fire which aroused them like they had never experienced before. Their fingers slow danced down their chests onto that plateau just above their belts, the leather exciting an urgency they hadn't felt up to this moment. Each wrapped their palm around the other's belt and pulled until they released. They looked into each other's eyes to check for permission and their smiles crinkled the edges into encouragement

Fingers found the clasp of waistbands and easily slid them to release. The anticipation of releasing zippers sent more shivers up their arms. As zippers lowered, the shivers intensified. Their hands slid inside and without ever asking, they each chose to slide their hands across the side of the underwear and marvel at the tautness of the muscles as they stood there. As they searched out the buttock, they caused the pants to shimmy down and puddle at their ankles. They stepped alternately freeing their feet. They caressed the cloth covered flesh and felt the full urgency as their erections strained the limits of the threads. They embraced and lowered onto the mattress, one leading the other with alternating gentle dominance guiding them. They wanted to savour the full force of expectancy and their libidos lavished them with sensations bringing them, each, to the outer limits of their ecstasy. They eased back and explored the sensations as they slid their bodies in rhythmic undulations bringing out the nuances created when hard muscles and flesh sing with the sensations of being pressed together through their boxer briefs.

They were so close, almost too close, but could that even be possible? The exhilaration they experienced closed their eyes and threw their heads back in savouring the delight. Their hands explored inside, and they felt the cloth tickle the hairs on the back of their hands as hot flesh excited their palms. They each slid the briefs down until they lay completely exposed. Their passion was driving them to a depth of pleasure they couldn't have known, but in that moment, it felt as natural as breathing. They connected at a primal level and explored that new excitement. How could they make this last? They barely touched. Their fingertips lightly stroked, and their tongues explored creating an increasing urgency until they reached a crescendo together.

Matthew whispered, "Happy Valentine's Day!"

They kissed and held each other knowing they had just experienced something special, reserved only for those who love.

They drifted off to sleep.

Chapter 12

Since Alice had told Brock of her illness three weeks before, he visited every day; sometimes for ten minutes, sometimes for an hour or more, depending on her energy level. He made sure she always had fresh flowers in the places where he knew she could spend time.

The caregivers, following Alice's direction not to hide anything from him, would tell him about her day and anything they thought he should know. He had seen a huge difference in her and Alice explained that the cancer was growing very rapidly. Her doctor was monitoring the occupancy of Caring Hearts Hospice and she was ready to go when an opening came up.

Today, Alice had had a good day and was sitting up in her room in the comfortable chair Brock had helped Paula move in from the living room two weeks ago. "Oh Honey, your visit is the highlight of my day. I get such a joy out of seeing you." She patted the chair next to hers. "Come, sit here, and tell me what you did today."

Brock filled her in on the Valentines Party at *'the Manor'*. He explained the decorations in detail and showed her pictures on his phone. He talked about how school and life at *the Manor'* was going. "I'm slowly getting used to walking up your driveway so close to my old home, but I still miss my family no matter how badly they treated me. Weird isn't it?"

"It's not weird at all. You have experienced a major upheaval in your life. I remember when my family disowned me for marrying Benny, I missed the daily interaction terribly. Some days Benny would catch me crying and he asked me what he could do to help, but there was nothing he could do. It was during that time when I connected to the wisdom: *'I only have control of me and no one else.'*. It took me a while to realize it, but I finally came to understand that I could do nothing to make my family change; that had to be their decision and, unfortunately, they died before they could. Around that time, I also connected to: *'Don take life for granted for you never know how much life you will have.'*. After I saw their lives cut short, I never took life for granted although, there was time after my son, Danny, was killed when I sunk into a depression and I simply didn't care if I lived or died. Once I was out of that darkness, I was able to look back and see the uselessness I felt and decided I wouldn't live a useless life. I have worked hard to live to that decision."

. Brock nodded, "I think there is some light coming into my darkness. Mackenzie convinced Mom to go to the Pflag meetings I told you about and she attended the meeting with her. She asked me to stay away so Mom wouldn't have to concern herself if I was in the room. She even got Mom to start reading the book I left on the table when I was kicked out. She and Mom are doing a little discussion group between them and Mackenzie is really enjoying the insightful perspective Mom is coming up with, so I would say she is on her way. I expect more good will come from her education. Mom tried to get Dad involved, but he remains pig-headed and has dismissed the whole idea. It's good to know that at least Mom has opened up a bit."

"Give them time. It takes time to dismantle old beliefs and learn new things. I believe your mother will progress faster than your father, but I bet he will come along at some point; don't lose hope." As Alice finished that statement, she went quiet and Brock could see she went somewhere distant with her thoughts. After several seconds, she gave her head a shake and continued talking as if the break hadn't occurred. "Change is hard for people. My father was so pig-headed, to use your words, that I really believe he was convinced I was dead to him. I could guess that my mother and sisters would want to contact me, but they never did, and I blame my father for that. They wouldn't have dared to go against his word. He ruled that house with an iron fist and all things went the way he decided they would, or you suffered bad consequences."

Alice's eyes started drooping and Brock took that as the sign to leave. "Well, Mammie, I had better get going. I have lots of homework to do so I'll see you tomorrow. I love you!"

"I love you too, Honey!" She waved to him as he left the room. He talked to Valerie for a few minutes before he left.

Chapter 13

In the one month since the January Pflag meeting, Mackenzie saw a big difference in her mother's attitude about attending the February meeting. In January, she was filled with dread and fear, but tonight she hopped out of the car without hesitation and joined the other people walking into the meeting. This time there was no attempt at a disguise.

As Mackenzie walked into the meeting room, she saw her mother chatting with some of the parents who attended the previous meeting. Mackenzie watched in awe at the transformation that was taking place right before her eyes. She took her seat next to her mother and thought about the past four weeks. Martha devoured every page of Brock's book and they had some lively and deep philosophical discussions about homosexuality from a variety of perspectives. They had explored many topics from whether it was genetic to how different religions dealt with it to how well Brock hid his being gay. They often sought out other resources to round out topics and her mother actually went online and purchased some of the books the parents recommended at the last meeting. Her fear was subsiding, and her growth was remarkable. Mackenzie was looking forward to how she would participate in tonight's meeting.

The meeting started and Martha's turn came in the introductions. "Hi, my name is Martha and I'm the mother of a gay son. This is my second meeting and I need to thank all of you who shared last month when I sat here like a dead log. I didn't participate because I was terrified that I was a terrible mother. Since then, I have read books and discussed them with my daughter, and I am in a different place. I'm not completely there but I am feeling I'm definitely on my way."

When the topics came up for discussion, Martha was the first to speak up. "I would like to explore what causes someone to be gay." Several other participants offered possible topic and Martha found she was interested in all of them and was looking forward to digging in.

The meeting ended far too quickly for Martha until she realized Andrew had let it continue for half an hour beyond the normal ending because everyone was engaged and the discussions were so lively, he could barely get a word in edgewise.

Martha and Mackenzie walked out of the meeting energized with a real appetite to learn more. Mackenzie, although always very open to LGBT issues and accepting of the community, was able to expand her view on several of the areas that were discussed. A moment of pride emerged as she saw her mother, although still struggling, as someone who had done a lot of work in a very short time and made headway in accepting that Brock is gay. She had a renewed and hopeful view of her mom.

Although Martha went into the meeting with an open mind, she left with a new and improved mindset. She participated in every discussion, explored ideas and perspectives, dug deeper when she didn't understand, and helped bring the participants in the room to new levels of understanding as she acted on a personal challenge to grow in her knowledge. She listened to everything that was shared by participants and clarified anything she didn't understand often coming to a new and different perspective which surprised even her.

Martha made good on Mackenzie's request to attempt to share information with Grant and confided how he had responded the previous month when he found they had gone to a Pflag meeting and dismissed the notion that he might attend. She also told her that he had called Brock's book '*propaganda*' when he saw that she was reading it. She had explained that over the past month, when she brought anything up, he dismissed her saying that she didn't know what she was talking about. She admitted that she really wasn't surprised by his reaction, but she hadn't been ready, herself, to address it. Tonight, she is in a different head space. She made a solid commitment to herself over the past couple of weeks that if Grant wouldn't come to the meetings, she would share as much of what she learned with him as she could. Martha was determined to break through his almost impenetrable exterior and told Mackenzie that she had silently given Grant one more month to start his education before she used desperate measures.

On the drive home, they talked about the topics that were discussed and summarized the points that Martha would try to review with Grant. Martha asked Mackenzie if she could give her an hour or so with him before coming home. Mackenzie agreed and after dropping Martha at home, she went to visit a friend.

Grant was watching TV when she entered the house. She didn't stop to say hello but went straight to the kitchen and started making tea. He had seen her go by and felt the change in routine. She always would stop and say hello, but for some reason tonight, she didn't. He turned off the show he was watching and went to the kitchen to see what was wrong. He found her sitting at the table reading and asked. "Where were you tonight?"

"You knew darned well that Mackenzie and I went to the Pflag meeting because I invited you to go with us."

Grant heard the attack; his face flushed, and he went on the defensive. "I'm not going to spend my Friday nights sitting in a room full of paedophiles."

She stood and positioned herself within a foot of him. "So, you jump right into your ignorant and vile stereotyping. You need to start understanding the LGBT community a whole lot better that you do, for your son's sake."

"Stop with this '*for your son's sake*' garbage. Everyone knows gay men are child molesters. I didn't make that up."

"At the meeting we had a father of a gay son who asked a question around that knowledge as you suggest. I don't know where you get your data, but I can guess it isn't backed by sound scientific research. Studies show that ninety per cent of child molesters are straight. I would like you to consider this…"

Grant interrupted. "You're not going to stand there and quote a bunch of Pflag bullshit, again are you? Well, I am not having it!" He thumped his fist down onto the counter and turned to walk away.

Martha reached out and took a hold on his shoulder and turned him around to face her. "Stop being so rude; you interrupted me. Please let me finish. What I was about to bring out is that a generally accepted figure is that ten per cent of the population is gay. If we accept that percentage, then ten per cent of teachers are gay, ten per cent of police officers are gay, ten per cent of firefighters are gay, ten per cent of ministers are gay, ten per cent of doctors are gay, ten per cent of masons are gay and so on through any group there is, so that would mean that ten per cent of child molesters are gay. Given that research doesn't support your generalization that all gays are child molesters, I would say it's more bullshit than what I just said. The other thing you need to get out of that is the other 90 per cent of child molesters are straight. What do you say about that, '*Mr. I think I know everything*'?"

Grant ignored her scoring a point for research and purposely switched topics. "What is with you swearing?"

Martha was ready for this and wasn't going to let Grant get to her. "You have been swearing as long as I can remember so I thought I would stoop to your level and maybe I would get something into that thick head of yours. When in Rome…."

"Well, I don't like it."

Martha jumped right on that without hesitation. "So, stop already. You have complete control over what you say."

"You're so sure of yourself, aren't you?"

"Yes, I'm quite sure that I'm on the right road to put this family back together. Our son is gay and I am educating myself, so I understand the world he has to live in. I want to create a safe and supportive environment for him, and I need you to join Mackenzie and me on this journey."

"I don't think you have heard me. Brock isn't gay, he just thinks he is, and at some point, he will choose not to be gay. Then and only then will I welcome him back into our family."

"Who hasn't heard whom? Your idiotic logic could be quite laughable if our family wasn't suffering because of it. Do you even hear yourself? What you spout as fact is nothing but pure ignorance. You need to educate yourself and reading the book Brock gave us would be a great start. I beg you to do something before you lose your family altogether."

"I've had enough of your drama. Go to your meetings if you must but leave me out of it. I am right. It has been almost six weeks so it shouldn't be too much longer before Brock sees the error to his ways. Mark my words." Grant turned and walked back into the living room.

Martha stood in the wake of his rebuff and watched him leave. The television started up and she shook her head in disbelief. '*This is going to be even tougher than I ever thought. Am I ready to bring out the big guns?*'

Chapter 14

Martha had been reading her book and looking things up on the Pflag Canada website. She marveled that all this information was right in front of her and she knew nothing about any of it. She admonished herself, '*I could have been learning about this for others in my life, but I assumed I was informed. I was only informed with information I got from uninformed people and I took their misinformation as fact.*' She was adamant about educating herself. She thought of others and Grant was first to mind. '*How many people accept misinformation as fact, like I have done, without ever educating themselves?*' The thought gave her a new perspective about society in general and the need that people not accept things without checking the facts. '*How many decisions that affect people's lives are made with misinformation presented as fact like the decision we made about Brock?*'

When Martha mulled things over, she liked to be on the move; she believed it helped her with her thinking. She often walked from room to room, up and down stairs, and tonight was no different. She was in her bedroom for the third time in her walk and, as she looked out the window, she saw movement around Mrs. DesRoches' home and thought. '*That must be Brock.*' Since that first time a week ago, she decided she would look every chance she could. It meant a lot for her to see even that little bit of Brock.

She focused on the movement, saw Brock walking out, and assumed he was heading to '*the Manor*'. Mackenzie had told her that Alice was ill, and it touched her heart to see Brock so dedicated to her. She wished he was here visiting her, but she knew that would come in time. She decided it was time she visit Alice and called over.

Valerie answered, "The DesRoches residence."

"Is Alice there?"

"Let me check and see if she is feeling up to taking a call."

Valerie checked with Alice and she took the call. "Hello, Alice here."

"Hi Alice, this is Martha. I heard you were ill and I was wondering if you're feeling well enough for a short visit?"

"Martha, what a lovely surprise; if you come over now, I could see you. My cancer makes me tire easily, but I'm feeling energetic at the moment. I just don't know how long it will last."

"I will be right there." She hung up the phone, wrapped up a bread she had made and threw on a coat.

Valerie answered the back door and Martha introduced herself, "Hi, I'm Martha Matheson from next door. I just called and Alice said I could come over. I brought this bread for her to enjoy."

"Thank you, I'm sure she will. My name is Valerie; I'm one of Alice's caregivers. You must be Brock's mother, am I right?"

"Yes, he is my son and he and Alice connected when he was a young boy; they have developed a close and special relationship."

"They certainly have. He doesn't miss a day of visiting her. She loves his visits and I'm glad he is in her life; there aren't too many other people who visit. Come this way."

In all the years they lived next door, she had only been in this house a couple of times. She looked around as she followed Valerie and took in the tired décor from years gone by. She entered the bedroom, "Hi Alice, how are you feeling?"

I am not well and tire easily but I think I have enough energy to enjoy a short visit."

I brought you one of my cinnamon apple breads, I know how you liked them."

"What a treat! You used to make them when I minded the kids. I loved the flavours; I can hardly wait to have a piece." Alice licked her lips and made smacking sounds. "Mmmmmmmmmm, I can taste it already!"

Martha was pleased with Alice's reaction. "I stopped making them years ago and only recently found the recipe. I hope you enjoy it."

"I know I will. Martha, I don't want you to think I am rude, but at any time I could become quite tired, so, if I end our visit, it's because of me, not you."

"Oh Alice, I completely understand."

Alice knew she would tire easily, but she knew how important this visit was. She mustered the energy to say what she needed to say. "I have been thinking about you since Brock moved out and was wondering how you were doing. Just so you know, I saw the awful fight, by chance. I was walking through my dining room when the glow of the candles on his birthday cake caught my attention and I turned my head to look. I saw more than I wanted to and, well, the rest is history."

Martha was a bit surprised with Alice's revelation. "I suppose Brock filled you in. I'm having a hard time, but I have made a commitment to put our family back together."

"I don't know if you knew, but I lost my only child, Danny, to an accident more than 60 years ago and I have missed him every day since. If I could go back and redo that day, I would, but I can't. Your son is a wonderful young man any parent would be proud to call their own, but your husband said he was dead to you both. Brock is very much alive, and I encourage you to do what you can to repair things. I know he wants to be part of your family again but only if he is accepted for who he is."

Martha had to know what Alice knew. "Did he share why this happened?"

"Yes, because he is gay. I suspected that he was for a few years now and I finally asked him the night he helped put up my Christmas tree."

Martha had never talked about Brock being gay. She didn't know what to say and was unsure of where to go with the conversation. "You knew?"

"Yes, for quite a while. Think about who Brock is; he is quite the catch. He has never had a girlfriend but not because the girls weren't interested. I watched him at the football games I went to and he seemed to be oblivious to the throngs of beautiful girls trying to get his attention. I put it together and waited for him to tell me, but my time is running out, so I decided to ask him."

Martha's surprise was palpable, "You are more astute than I am; I never saw it at all."

Alice sighed, "Sometimes we just don't want to see some things. As I said, I do not have much time left and I want the best for your son. Please promise me you will open yourself to learn about your son's world and be there to support him when others lash out against him. The world can be a nasty place and he will need his mother."

Martha thought about what Alice said. "I'm trying, but it isn't easy."

Alice looked her in the eyes and gave her some wisdom, "It is only hard if you make it so. All you have to do is love him unconditionally; he really is quite lovable. You only have control of yourself, no one else. Choose to truly love him."

Martha started to tear up, "I will. I promise. Thank you, Alice."

"I guess I overdid it and now I need to sleep. Thank you for your visit Martha; I had wanted to talk to you about Brock but didn't want to intrude." Alice's eyes drooped a few times and then closed. Martha went to the kitchen.

"She is a very wise woman." Martha said to Valerie as she put on her coat.

"Yes, we have wonderful talks. I feel truly blessed to be able to care for such a wonderful soul."

Chapter 15

The next day, Mackenzie popped in about eleven thirty and Gregory invited her to stay for lunch. "You catch up with Brock and we will get lunch ready. If you need privacy, you have the whole house to choose from as all the guests are out."

Mackenzie wanted to update Brock on the happenings in the family, but she trusted the guys. "Thanks guys, but we can catch up here and I think you'll want to hear today's update anyway. This morning at breakfast, after Dad had left, Mom told me about seeing you leave Mammie's last night and she decided to visit, so I pumped her for details." Mackenzie replayed everything she knew and then asked, "How do you like being the centre of attention?"

"I'm slowly getting used to it. What caused Mom to visit Mammie? Did she say?"

"I think it came out of a conversation I had with her the other day." Mackenzie thought back, "Oh, I remember. She told me she saw you coming out of Mammie's house and asked me how often you visited her. I told her about Mammie's cancer, and she hadn't heard anything about it. I guess I never mentioned it because I'm on strike talking about you to them. I want it to be so uncomfortable that they realize what they did disowning you. Did I ever tell you I can be stubborn?" Mackenzie grinned.

"No! Not you!" Brock smirked and then got serious. "So she saw me visiting Mammie. Well, I'm glad she visited, and I can just bet that Mammie gave her an earful. She would do it nicely, but she wouldn't hold back. She is mad at them for hurting me."

Mackenzie nodded, "That she is, and her words really got Mom thinking so I think a lot of good will come out of that visit. Mom didn't know about Danny, her son that died."

"I'm not surprised. It happened before Mom and Dad were born so it would have been old news and something painful that one wouldn't bring up to anyone."

Mackenzie jumped on that, "Old news or not, that info hit Mom hard. The fact that

Mammie lost her son because he died, and Mom lost you because of a decision. Mammie brought that home to her. Mammie told Mom that she has a choice, and she could have you back in her life whereas nothing Mammie could do would bring her son back into her life."

Andrew and Gregory brought plates of food over and handed them out before sitting down. Andrew spoke, "I can't help thinking of the power of that comparison. She made a strong point; death has no reverse position."

Brock interjected, "And Mom and Dad can reverse their decision anytime. Would they have felt worse if I died?"

Gregory joined the discussion, "You do have a point but let's not go there. As Andrew spoke, I wondered how many parents 'kill off' their child with the threat of being kicked out or disowned, all the time knowing the decision could be reversed. Is it simply a manipulative threat that parents use?"

"I've never considered killing myself but there are many teens who do commit suicide because they are afraid of being rejected by their family. For me, Dad did say that I could be in the family if I chose not to be gay, but I have had enough dishonesty. I needed to be me, not someone I made up for their acceptance."

Andrew added. "And everyone chooses what is best for them given the circumstances. You have high integrity Brock and I admire you for that. I know you have paid dearly but I believe you are the catalyst to some big changes that your family will go through. They will emerge from that process as better people. I find it hard to believe that parents find having a gay child to be more unacceptable than kicking their child out or disowning them. Where is their sense of family, or of basic right and wrong?"

Mackenzie chimed in, "I guess it is all part of their evolution on their life's journey. I just hoped Mom and Dad had evolved enough to accept Brock. I was wrong. Brock, how do you think Mammie is doing? Mom thought she was feeble and didn't look so good."

He gave his full attention to his answer. "She is getting so frail and is tired all the time; it is difficult to get half an hour visit in before she drifts off. The doctor is on top of her meds so, for the most part, she is being kept as pain free as possible. The downside is that the meds make her tired. It's a fine line. She has given her doctor the go ahead for her to go to Caring Hearts Hospice when a bed becomes open. I hope it will be soon."

"Does she have all of her affairs in order?" Andrew asked.

"She hasn't mentioned them to me. She is a very organized person, so I'm assuming she does."

Chapter 16

Mammie called before Brock left for school and told him that Caring Hearts Hospice had a room for her and shared, "Honey, I will be moving over later this morning, as soon as they can arrange transportation. Will you come visit me once I get settled in?"

Brock replied, "Mammie, nothing would keep me away. I have been checking the bus routes and there is a bus stop right across the street. I will call to make sure you are admitted and then I will be over."

"Oh Honey, I can save you a call. Paula will call you when she has me all unpacked and situated. I will see you later. Love you!"

"That would be perfect! I love you too Mammie!"

On his way to 'the Manor' for lunch, Paula called. He asked her to tell Mammie that he would visit her right after school. He updated the guys on Mammie and that he was going over after school so he would be home for a late supper.

During the bus ride, the late-February sun shone on Brock most of the way over and he enjoyed the warmth as he thought about Mammie. He saw the Caring Hearts Hospice sign before the bus stopped and was relieved that he had found it so easily.

He was all aquiver as he walked toward the building. It loomed over him and the reality sunk in. He couldn't wrap his head around what to expect of a place where people go to die. All the sadness he was expecting made him question if he would be able to handle the visits. What he did know was that no matter what, he would overcome his reticence so he could see his Mammie.

He followed the signs and found the elevator. The ride felt like it took forever. At one point in the ride, he questioned whether the elevator was working. When the doors opened, he stepped into a hallway in front of a desk. A couple of staff looked up and one asked if she could help him.

"I'm here to visit Alice DesRoches."

The staff member responded. "She is in Room six right over there, but before you do see her, I need you to sign in. This log tells us who is in the building in case of emergencies, so we get all visitors to sign in when they arrive and out when they leave."

"Thank you." He signed in and turned, but saw the room was darkened so he turned back and asked, "Is she sleeping?"

"The sun was bright earlier today, so we closed the blinds. We should be able to open them now. I was just in and she was watching TV." Seeing his name as he signed in, she asked, "Are you the Brock Matheson who we have on record as her next of kin?"

"Yes, that's me."

"Nice to meet you and put a face to a name. My name is Tammy. Please let one of us know if she is experiencing any discomfort. We want every patient to be comfortable so if she needs anything, we can help. Also, if you have any questions, please ask. Is this your first time at Caring Hearts Hospice?"

"Yes, I know very little about it."

"Would you like a tour? Things are all caught up and people are resting, so this would be a great time."

"Thanks, can she come on the tour?"

"Yes, I will get her a wheelchair."

Alice's face took on a rosy glow when she saw him. "Oh Honey, thank you for coming, I was laying here missing you."

"Hi Mammie, how are you doing so far?"

"I couldn't be treated any better. This is a delightful place. Look at this room; it is so bright and cheery, I love it! The people who work here are wonderful and caring. It seems I have met everyone working today. They all stopped in and asked if I needed anything. I feel like royalty!"

"That is wonderful! Remember, if you need anything from the outside, just call me, and I will bring it with me."

"I know you would, but I don't want to be too much of a bother."

"Please believe me, you are never a bother. How are you feeling?"

"I wish I could say wonderful, but I would be lying, so would 'okay' work?"

"If you're uncomfortable, Tammy told me we just ask her for something to help so don't hesitate. Are you in pain now?"

"Not at this time."

"Okay, would you like to go for a tour of this place? Tammy offered one if we were interested. She is getting you a wheelchair right now."

"That would be lovely."

Tammy brought the wheelchair and Brian, the PSW, helped Alice into it. Brock took her around the floor, and she noted some changes that had taken place since she had visited friends a couple of years ago. She was impressed with the chapel on the first floor being non-denominational. They ended up in the family sitting rooms at the front of the building and she remarked how much like a house it was. He could see the tour was taking its toll. Her eyes were drooping, so he took her back to her room and got Brian to put her in bed.

Brock sat next to Alice as she recalled memories of her childhood he hadn't heard before. She gave examples of how stern and regimental her father was and how obedient her mother was when he was around. She also shared that, while her father was away travelling, her mother would do things he had expressly forbidden. She had made a game out of it with '*this will be our little secret.*' and got the girls to promise not to tell.

Mammie and Brock played games of asking each other '*what if*' questions. In one round, Alice asked, "What if you had lots of money, what would you do?"

Brock responded after careful thought, "I think I would open a place for people who were kicked out of their home or needed to get away from it. I can't imagine where I would be today if it wasn't for the support I received from Andrew, Gregory and you. I often wonder what people do when they don't have that support, so I would like to give them a safe place to land."

"What a lovely thought! I remember when my parents kicked me out, I had Benny, but now that you say it, where would people go at times like that?"

"I think that's why we have homeless people or people committing suicide. They have nowhere to turn and they must be so desperate. Okay, my turn, what if you could change anything in your life, what would it be?"

"I have thought about that most of my life. I would have forbidden Danny to play on the snowbank. I was watching him from the living room window and thought it was dangerous, but never acted on my thought. I would change that." Her eyes watered and tears flowed down her cheek. "I really believe everything happens for a reason but getting anything positive out of Danny's death was the hardest thing I ever did."

"You got something positive out of it?"

"Yes. When he died, I went into a severe depression and Benny, God rest his soul, tried everything to break its hold on me. Eventually, he brought a rose bush home and made me go with him into the back yard that had nothing but weeds and we planted that bush. He would take me out every night, week after week, and talk me through caring for it; he relinquished his ownership and shifted the care over to me bit by bit until it gave me a reason to live. We'll never know for sure, but I have often reflected on whether I would have taken to gardening on my own. So, because my son died, I got into gardening and because of gardening, I met you. Our souls mingled around planting and nourishing that back yard. Everything happens for a reason and I believe our relationship is that reason."

Just then there was a knock. A gentleman who Brock hadn't seen before stepped into the room.

"Good to see you Wade, come in. Brock, this is Wade Jackson, my Power of Attorney and Executor of my estate. He has all of my plans for my funeral."

Brock was still getting used to Alice's pragmatic way of addressing, what could be, a sensitive issue. "It's nice to meet you, Mr. Jackson." They shook hands.

"Call me Wade. Here's my information if you need to contact me. There are a few things I need to discuss with Alice if you could give us ten minutes or so."

"Sure, I'll go out to the family room." Brock excused himself and had been in the family room about twenty minutes when he saw Wade waiting by the elevator. "Mr. Jackson, um, I mean Wade, is she resting?"

"She was quite spry while we talked over some things, but was getting droopy, so I said goodbye and left."

"I guess I will be seeing you at the funeral. It is so surreal to even be saying that."

"I know. She is quite the lady and is ready to go." The elevator doors opened, and he stepped in, holding the doors from closing as he said his parting words. "It was nice meeting you Brock. Alice thinks the world of you. She tells me you have been like the son she doesn't have. Let me know if you need me."

"Thank you Wade, she is very special to me. Bye."

When Brock went back to the room, Alice was sleeping peacefully. As he looked at her and wondered what the end would look like. He started to tear up when she opened her eyes.

"Hello Honey, did I sleep long?"

He dabbed his eyes. "Not long."

"I tire so easily; they tell me that is caused by the cancer and the drugs. It's almost supper time, so you need to get yourself back to 'the Manor'. Is it starting to feel like home yet?"

"No, it's a wonderful place and the guys have been more than supportive, but it isn't my home yet." His answer surprised him, and he hesitated for a few seconds thinking about what home really is. "You rest up and I'll be back tomorrow. Remember, if there is anything you want, just give me a call."

"I will; you are sweet. I love you, Honey." As she said the last words, her eyes drooped, and her head rolled to one side. It startled Brock how fast she changed, and he found himself watching her chest as it rose and fell to make sure she was breathing. Although it took what seemed like forever, she was breathing, and it gave him some level of comfort. Just to make sure, he backed out of her room as he left so he could monitor the motion of her breathing.

Chapter 17

Kyle was waiting for Brock when he arrived at school, "Trevor should arrive this afternoon. How do your evenings look for that supper we talked about?"

"Oh, Kyle, with everything that has been going on I forgot all about Trevor and the supper. Sorry." He had been actually looking forward to seeing Trevor again, so he was surprised he had forgotten. "Mammie is dying of cancer and has been admitted to Caring Hearts Hospice. I go over after school every day and stay with her until she goes to sleep for the night. I won't be able to go to supper with you. How about we meet at 'the Manor' around eight-thirty."

A look of panic clouded Kyle's face. "Can we meet somewhere other than 'the Manor'?"

"Kyle, the guys aren't perverts, like you say, it will be fine."

"Brock, I can't go to 'the Manor'. The owners have a restraining order on me, and I cannot set foot on their property."

"When did that happen?"

"Early last year around the time you were hired."

"What does my hiring have to do with your restraining order?"

"It seems they have security cameras and caught me on video ringing the doorbell and taking off."

"Did they catch you spray painting the graffiti?"

"They didn't have the cameras then. That was late April of last year and I went back three or four more times in May after that. I guess they installed the cameras that caught me in the act. They showed the police, but I wasn't known to them. They needed to identify me somehow before they could catch me. When I interviewed for the job, they remarked that I looked familiar, but couldn't place me. That is, until right after my interview. One of them couldn't let it go and then it dawned on him that I could be the guy on the video. It is very clear and when they looked that night, they were sure it was me. They contacted the police and gave them my name and address from my résumé, so the police came to my home. Mom freaked. The owners could have charged me, but thankfully they just wanted me to stop, so I agreed to a restraining order."

Brock was interested, "Did they bring up the graffiti?"

"The police mentioned the graffiti and said they suspected I did it. They told me how it was considered a hate crime and what the penalty was if I was found guilty. I'm glad you got so pissed at me because it made me think and that was the only time I did it. Luckily, the owners didn't pursue it with the police."

Brock had a thoughtful look on his face as he shook his head, "It all makes sense now. How about meeting at Tim Hortons on Waterloo Street?"

"Trevor and I can have supper and then meet you there. Does eight thirty, work?"

"That should work well. Right now, I'd better get to class. See you tonight!"

*****

After school, Brock went home to drop his things before he headed over to Caring Hearts Hospice.

He was up in his room when he heard footsteps on the stairs that stopped outside his door. He waited for the knock and opened it right away. Trevor stood there looking as handsome as ever. They threw their arms around each other and hugged.

"It is good to see you, Brock. The guys have filled me in on all that has been happening in your world. I was wondering why the emails had stopped about a month ago, but I now understand why."

"Sorry Trevor, I told you about the important things and then life got crazy."

"Yes, you told me about your boyfriend, Matthew. I hope I get to meet him. You also told me about being kicked out and I thank my lucky stars I didn't come out to my parents. I don't know how it could be possible, but I imagine it would be worse with them."

"That would mean you would be dead. Anyway, everything after that is a blur. I was supposed to go to supper with you and Kyle, but ..."

"I know, Kyle explained it to me. I guess we are meeting later."

"Only for Kyle's benefit. Have you told him anything about us?"

"Oh, Brock. I would never out someone, at least not intentionally. No, Kyle knows we met here while you were working, but I kept details generic. He doesn't even know we email each other."

"Thank you. Kyle can be quite a homophobe and I worried he would use it against me. Are you out to him?"

"Heavens no; that would too close to home and Kyle doesn't keep much to himself. We are like brothers, but we certainly do not share everything."

"Thank you. I trusted you wouldn't, but Kyle just gave me a vibe that he knew more than he was saying."

"If he does, it didn't come from me. So, do you have a few minutes to fill me in on the things the guys wouldn't know?"

"There isn't much that the guys don't know about me." He started telling Trevor about his life since being kicked out; Mammie's health, school, his family and the progress or lack of progress they were making.

Trevor filled him in on his life and told Brock he was ready to move on from Boston. "I think I might try Halifax."

They talked until Brock had to leave. He hugged Trevor. "I guess we will meet tonight and share light items where we hardly know one another."

"Right and Kyle will take over the conversation, so we have no worries. Whatever questions he asks about us, the first one to answer it will be supported by the other. Agreed?"

"Agreed! See you later!"

Chapter 18

The sun had set and Martha stood in the dining room window looking out at the moonlight reflected on the snow. She thought about Brock sliding in that driveway as a kid and him always being over at Alice's house. She wondered if he would be at '*the Manor*' tonight. It was funny for her to think of any other place as Brock's home. It has been just over two months since his fateful birthday when he stormed out of the ruckus in the very room she was standing because he was told he was dead to them. Grant really was the one to say it, but she didn't do anything to change it, so she was just as guilty.

The Pflag meetings she had attended with Mackenzie had opened her eyes to a different gay world than she had been told. So much has changed for her and now she wanted to explore more with Brock present; she wanted to know the real Brock, maybe for the first time since he was a kid. Mackenzie offered to ask him, but she needed to take this first step and ask him herself if he would come to tomorrow's meeting. She hadn't contacted him in two months but thought about it every day. Not talking to her son told her things about the kind of mother she was, and they weren't nice things. She didn't like herself for allowing this to happen. She contemplated calling and was desperate to speak to him, but really wanted to see him in person. The turmoil in her stomach kept her looking out the window and she seized the moment and marched to the hall in a purposeful stride, grabbed her coat and walked out the door before her stomach stopped her again. No matter what happened, she would go to 'the Manor' and ring that doorbell. She hoped Brock would answer.

She took her car and arrived faster than she expected. As she mounted the front stairs her stomach did a flop, but she was determined to talk to him, and she ignored everything but the lighted doorbell. She pressed it and let go of the breath she had been holding.

Brock opened the door, and his eyes went wide but focused on her. "Hi Mom", he hesitated, "Is it okay to still call you Mom or am I still dead to you?"

Martha burst into tears as she engulfed her son in a big hug. "You are my son, and I am your mother and I never again want anything to ever change that."

Brock participated in the hug because he needed it but kept his guard up. He was cold. "Come in Mom. It has been a while and I think we need to talk." He took her coat and hung it up. "Would you like some tea?"

"I would love some, if you will join me."

"Love to." They went to the kitchen, filled the kettle and while it was heating up, he went through the tea choices he had and they both selected the same Apple Cinnamon one. He got two mugs from the cupboard, made the tea, and sat across from each other at the table.

Martha was hesitant when she asked, "Are the owners home?"

"No, they are out for the evening. We have two guests, but they won't be bothering us."

"Good, we need to talk, and I don't want to have to deal with anyone else. Son, I don't know how you could forgive me, but I have learned a lot from the Pflag meetings, and I know that your dad and I were wrong. I want you to come to tomorrow's meeting so we can air our differences in a safe environment and learn from each other. Would you do that for me?"

"Yes, I will do that but there will be benefit for both of us. I attended the Pflag meetings last fall to get my head together about being gay. All the garbage Dad spewed had a negative effect on me. He really believes he knows what he is talking about, but he is so far off. Those meetings helped in saving my sanity and prepared me to come out to you and Dad."

"I have been sharing what I have learned with your father, but he is slow to change. I don't know what it will take, but your sister is relentless in telling him he is wrong among other things; none of them good. I don't know what else he needs to hear to move him in the right direction."

"Mom, does Dad know you are here tonight?"

"No, I did this on my own. Your father and I are on different paths, but I want to be on your path."

Brock took each of her hands in his and looked her in the eyes. "I cannot be teased like this, Mom. Either you're in my life or you're out of it. What will it be?"

"I'm in. Let me deal with Dad. He may not like it, but I won't lose you again. If he insists, I may have to move out to prove a point." She smiled at the thought.

"I need to visit Mammie at Caring Hearts Hospice first, but I will be there tomorrow. Mom, is it okay to tell you I love you for this?"

"Thank you! I needed to hear that so badly. I don't want you to ever feel you can't tell me something. I promise I will always listen like a mother should."

*****

Brock visited Mammie after school and told her all about his mother's visit. He finished his visit in time to catch the bus to the Pflag meeting, arriving just as it was about to start.

There were no new people at the meeting, so introductions were simple. Martha's was the exception. Although the people in the room had heard most of what she was going to say, she wanted Brock to hear her. "My name is Martha and I'm the mother of a gay son. Two months ago, he came out to us at his birthday celebration and my husband kicked him out of our home telling him he wasn't welcome back until he decided not to be gay. At the time, I was in a blur, and my silence to what was going on supported my husband and I lost a part of me that I have been mourning every day since. I asked my son if he would come tonight so that we can learn from each other in a safe environment; I need help, so I don't mess this up. I want to learn, I want him in my life, and I want to be the loving, supportive mother I have failed to be."

Brock spoke next, "My name is Brock and I'm her gay son. I'm here to make things right between us and help Mom understand my truest version of me."

Mackenzie went after Brock. "I'm Mackenzie, Brock's sister. I'm here to support both my mother and my brother and have wanted tonight to happen ever since our family was torn apart."

The rest of the introductions concluded, and Andrew spoke to the room. "We have an opportunity to hear a mother and son discuss a very delicate issue from which I think we could all learn. I also want to know if there are any other issues we need to discuss tonight."

There was silence as people thought about what was to happen when Breanne, the transgender daughter, looked at her mother and then the room and said, "I think we'll all learn something, and I welcome Martha and Brock doing what they need to do."

"Anyone have anything else?" Andrew asked and was answered with heads all around the room. "Okay Martha, the floor is yours."

Martha was wringing a pair of leather gloves in her hands, looked at her son and started talking, "From attending the past two Pflag meetings I have had a hard look at myself and I have to say I'm not proud of how we treated you, Brock. You are our son and we have failed you. As your parents, we were supposed to support you as you grew into a healthy, happy, well-adjusted, independent adult and when I think of what we did more than two months ago, I am embarrassed and very ashamed."

Brock looked directly into Martha's eyes and spoke. "Mom, to be truthful, it has been more than a few months; it has been years. My birthday is when you became aware. All my knowing life, I knew I was different, but didn't have the gay label until later when I heard the bigoted slurs Dad would make when I was young about the people fighting for gay rights; rights he already had because he was heterosexual. It scared me to think gay and I did everything

I could to not be gay, but I wasn't being me. You and Dad brought us up," he paused to look at his sister before continuing, "to be honest people and yet your behaviours told me I had to hide who I was from you. I had to live a lie to receive your love. I carried the fear of losing my family, my friends, and my world and your behaviours reinforced those fears. They forced me into a dishonesty that didn't feel right. I learned that if I wanted to be in the family, I had to be a different person, one you and Dad would accept."

Martha's face twisted and tears sprouted from the corners of her eyes. She didn't wipe them away, instead, she let them flow freely as a kind of unspoken penance.

Brock continued, "When it became too much for me, I came out. The first person I had to come out to was me. I had denied it for so long that to actually say the words was the hardest thing I had to admit to myself. Someone came into my life who helped me feel good about being me and accepted me in my honesty. I then came out to people who I trusted wouldn't reject me, Mackenzie, Andrew, and Gregory. I'm so thankful they supported me, and I experienced unconditional love; a love I had never felt before. Then Mammie shocked me when she guessed and was, again, kind and unconditionally loving. I couldn't believe an old lady of ninety-eight would be able to accept something my parents, who are about half her age, couldn't. I told myself that I couldn't come out to you because you wouldn't be able to accept me for who I am. I was afraid, but with the positive responses I had from people who love me to bolster my resolve, I decided to be honest with you. Mackenzie and I prepared for all possible reactions around how you and Dad would respond, but nothing would have prepared me for the moment Dad said words that have been etched into my being: '*As long as you insist on being gay, I do not want you as my son – you are dead to me and are no longer welcome in my home. Get out!*' I, not only, couldn't believe I was being kicked out of the only home I had ever known, but that I was dead to him for being gay. How can you as a mother wrap your head around that? I lost respect for you when you did nothing to counter his hate-filled words and allowed me to walk out. Where was my mother? I thought you loved me."

Martha broke into quiet sobbing. She took several tissues, wiped her eyes and blew her nose. She sat back in an exhausted slump with shoulders sagging under the weight of what she heard. "Oh Brock, I hurt for the pain we have caused you and if I could have a magical wish, I would go back to that night and support you with the unconditional love you deserve. To know your father's hateful words will be with you forever is nothing less than emotional abuse and no person should have to experience such hatred and bigotry, especially a child of mine. I do not have magic and we cannot go back, but as Mackenzie often says, life presents us with learning opportunities, and we need to turn this into a major learning. I get it now, but if in the future I behave as if I haven't, I give you full permission to take me to task. I love you and want you in my life. The learning I'm getting will be shared with your father and he will be at the next meeting or we'll not continue to be married. I will not accept any more of his ignorance and I will demand he open himself to learn. I have had a life of him giving ultimatums; now, it is my turn." The air hung heavy with her words and one person started to clap, then another and another until everyone was standing and applauding; all eyes were focused on Martha.

Brock pulled her out of her chair and wrapped his arms around her and whispered into her ear as the applause continued. "I love you so much, Mom!"

Chapter 19

Martha asked Mackenzie if she would take the car and go over to a friend's place so she could be alone with Grant.

Mackenzie questioned, "Are you going to be okay?"

"Don't you worry, I can handle myself." As she walked to the house, she was thinking about the best way to deal with him.

As she went in the back door, she could hear the TV. Grant was watching one of his shows, but not for much longer. She walked into the living room and Grant didn't take his eyes from the TV, but spoke, "How was the meeting?"

She hadn't told him about Brock attending, but everything was coming out tonight. She walked over and turned the TV off. Grant looked at her, "What the hell are you doing; that's my show." He clicked the remote and the TV came back to life.

Martha walked over and pulled the plug out of the wall. "You can watch that show about fake lives anytime. We need to talk about real life, our life. Now!"

Grant noted her tone and when he looked at her, he saw that her facial muscles were rigid. He knew they would be talking, so he gave up any hope of seeing his show. "Ok, what do we need to talk about?"

"We're going to talk about our family, our whole family. Last night, I went to see Brock and asked him to attend tonight's meeting, which he did. I wanted to listen to his story and hear him and I heard him in spades. I cannot find the words to adequately tell you how embarrassed and ashamed I am with your treatment of him and, if it's possible, I am more embarrassed that I sat back and allowed it to happen. The hateful bigotry you have for gay people is pure, unfounded ignorance and….."

Grant jumps up from his chair, took a step toward Martha and spoke louder interrupting what she was saying. "How dare you speak to me like…"

Martha took a deliberate step forward, raised her voice and didn't allow him to finish his statement. "Like I was saying, you need an education. You're making a fool out of yourself adhering to the ignorance you spew. I'm done pussyfooting around you and I refuse to take your judgements for truth anymore. I have educated myself and I expect you to educate yourself. Contrary to your belief, gay isn't a disease that can be cured or that someone can catch by hanging around other gay people. Also, someone doesn't decide to be gay; they can only decide to live true to who they are or to live a lie. That horrible ultimatum you gave Brock with 'As long as you insist on being gay….' was blatant ignorance. You think gay is a choice. You probably heard that from some, just as ignorant, radical religious fundamentalists who cannot think for themselves and I say that because it is not a choice. People are born the sexual orientation they are so, just like you were born heterosexual and it wasn't anything you could choose, Brock was born gay and it wasn't something he chose. Our genetics created him, so how can we punish our child for being who we created.

The environment that we created in our home made him feel he couldn't be who he is or he would be rejected. He was so right to fear that because we rejected him. I should have spoken to you long ago and we wouldn't be in this mess we have gotten our family into. I'm done being subservient to you. If you want to stay married to me, we're going to be equals and our home will be run with unconditional love and acceptance of who our children are. First, you're going to a therapist to find out why you need to feel superior to women, gays, or for that matter, anyone different from you. On top of that, you will be attending Pflag meetings with me going forward until you start to behave like I want my husband and the father of my children to behave."

"Are you through?"

"I have other things to say, but I need you to talk. You must think about what Mackenzie says. She hasn't minced words and her message is dead on, but you don't ever talk about it. She must be getting to you; if she isn't, your brain has to be numb. What is going on in that head of yours?"

"I don't know where to start."

"Try!"

"Do you think I haven't noticed that I'm standing alone on this issue and the lack of support hasn't gotten me to questioning things?"

"I hope you have, but you haven't spoken to me about anything; all you do is make fun of what I say, spout bigoted perspectives, and outright deny there is a problem. I need to know, are you proud that our son isn't part of our family?"

"No, I'm not proud, and I was hoping it would have been resolved by now."

"Well, it isn't resolved, and it will never be to your definition of resolved. Your ultimatum to Brock is so outrageous it cannot even start to happen unless Brock goes back in his closet and that will never happen because I have made a solemn vow to love my son unconditionally. That is why I am using ultimatums on you; that is how important it is to me. I don't want to continue living the way we have been living. You have to start coming to meetings and seeing a therapist." Martha was strong but losing steam. She had to assure herself she wouldn't give in to his lack of commitment.

"Alright, I'll meet you halfway. I'll go to your meetings, but I'm not going to a therapist; they are for crazy people."

"You think so! Well, I have been seeing a therapist for the past two months and I'm not crazy. If anything, I was crazy accepting your ignorance and bigotry for all these years."

Grant's eyes opened wide, "You've been seeing a therapist. You never mentioned it to me."

"Why would I? You would have made some ignorant remark that I didn't want to hear. Tonight, when Brock spoke, he talked about the fear he lived with every day that, if we knew who he really was, we would reject him. I think I can connect with the fear and when he spoke about it, I realized I have been hiding '*me*' all these years worried that you would reject me. I have been subservient to you because I thought that was who you wanted me to be. I worked so hard at being who you wanted me to be that I forgot to be me. Well, that's over; I'm coming out as a strong woman and not hiding anymore."

"Like you have been hiding so much." Grant huffed.

"I have, do you want a big example?" Martha smugly asked.

"Yeah, tell me one thing other than the therapist that you've been hiding."

"Do you know my yearly salary is three times what you make?"

"I would know that if that were true." Grant called her bluff.

"You think? I have been doctoring up my pay stubs, so you, the man in this relationship, could feel superior. I get the bulk of my pay taken out and invested so that my take-home amount is less than yours. You've only looked at the amount I bring home; the truth is in the deductions. I took the chance that the take-home amount is the only thing you cared about and wouldn't look at the deductions. That's hiding."

"You never let on." He was dazed by the revelation.

"No, I never let on. I was afraid you would find out and we would fight. I have also been hiding my intelligence; dumbing myself down for you. I'm very intelligent, actually MENSA intelligent, and have been hiding that from you our whole time together because mother pounded into my head that smart girls don't get a man. I would make sure we wouldn't have deep conversations, so I didn't bruise your fragile male ego. Our whole married life I have manufactured the wife I thought you wanted, and I'm fed up with it. I have made an appointment for you with my therapist for tomorrow morning at ten thirty. I've been thinking the only way our family will get back together is for you to deal with your issues and she is ready for you."

"I won't go."

"You think so, do you? Let me say it a different way. You seem to understand ultimatums, so if you want to stay married to me, you will go for therapy. I no longer want to be married to an over-bearing, ignorant, bigot who thinks any person who is different is lower than him. If we're going to be equals, you need therapy, so you choose."

"You can't be serious."

"I'm dead serious. I no longer want to be in this marriage if you do not want to become enlightened."

"What has gotten into you? You aren't the woman I married."

"Oh yes I am, I just didn't let you see her. So, if you don't want to be married to me anymore, here is your out!"

"Alright, I'll go to your therapist, but I won't like it."

"I don't need you to like it, I need you to do your work and become a decent husband and father. To do that you need to figure out why you need to put others down when they are different than you and why you fear them."

"I don't fear them."

"That isn't a conversation that we're going to have, but one you will be having with the therapist. She has a good understanding of who will be in her office in the morning, so you won't be able to ignore anything or try to pull the wool over her eyes. Her name is Anne Stokes and she is good."

Chapter 20

Grant arrived at the parking lot to the building with Anne Stokes' office and sat in his car wondering what he was doing. He reflected on what Martha had said the previous evening and didn't want to lose her, but he was completely uncomfortable with what he was about to do next. His hand fidgeted with the door latch, but he didn't pull it hard enough to release the locking mechanism. He kept looking to see if anyone saw that he was there. His only comfort was that the building contained offices for a variety of professionals, and no one could guess accurately which one he was about to visit. He watched the clock and he had to make a decision. He pulled the latch and the cold, March-morning air assaulted his face taking his mind off his queasy stomach.

Using Martha's directions, he found the office without much difficulty, but before stopping he looked in both directions checking for people. The hall was empty. Instead of turning the knob, he stood there holding it. Long minutes passed when he heard the elevator doors open down the hall. He turned and pushed the door open into the office to get out of sight. He stood facing an empty reception desk with a sign '*Please ring the bell and be seated.*' He rang, sat, and tried to find a magazine that would interest him, but before he could, the door opened and a tall, slim attractive, lady in her forties with blond hair in a stylish cut walked out.

Grant stood as she took long strides over to him with her hand extended.

When they connected, "Hi, my name is Anne Stokes, call me Anne. Are you my ten-thirty appointment?"

Grant was impressed at the strength of her grip, "Yes, I'm Grant Matheson and my wife booked this for me."

"Come into my office." She led the way to a set of comfortable chairs with a coffee table between and Grant took the seat she offered him. She sat and asked, "May I call you Grant?"

"Yes."

She waited for him to say more, but when nothing came, she opened with, "So, Grant, why are you here?"

"I thought you knew; didn't Martha tell you?"

"Martha told me why she thinks you need to be here, but I want to know why you are here."

Grant thought for a few minutes and Anne waited. "Martha told me she has been seeing you for a few months and she's finding it helpful. She then told me I needed therapy and if I wanted to stay married to her, I needed to see you, so here I am."

"When she told you that, how did you feel?"

"I guess I was mad. Just because she needs therapy doesn't mean everyone does."

"What made you mad?"

"I don't think I need therapy. I lead a pretty good life." Grant talked about his life in general and explained his world as he saw it.

"You said you have a pretty good life. Let's talk about what makes your life good. How do you think your marriage and family life is going?"

"We are having a few glitches right now, but overall, it is solid."

"Tell me about the glitches."

"Martha is a good wife, but she has gotten it into her head that I need to change and that is causing some friction. It all started when my son, Brock, told us he is gay, and I kicked him out."

"So, you see kicking your son out of your home as a glitch?"

"Everything was going well until that happened, so it is a glitch. Once we work on it, things will be back to normal." Grant talked about his life with Martha and the type of woman she was or, at least, who he thought she was and how things have changed so much. He went back to the day they met that started their dating and how he felt about her. He continued with the family coming along and how he was a great husband in his estimation. Then he came back to today's reality, "The problem right now is we are all at odds, well I am at odds with the other three. My daughter Mackenzie is very opinionated and supports her big brother being gay, so there is no talking to her. She has, somehow, convinced Martha that I am wrong and has gotten her mom to read books and go to meetings, so now Martha is convinced Brock really is gay and cannot change. I believe he is just confused, and it will just be a matter of time before he finds he isn't, but she won't listen to my reasoning. Basically, I think she is being brainwashed."

Anne knew from what Martha had told her that Grant would be a challenge, but she was stunned that his convictions were so strong. "You seem so sure of your reasoning. Where did you learn about homosexuality?"

Grant explained his "on the streets" education, his beliefs, and he mentioned the Bible, but basically offered no sound reference material. He added opinions, perspectives, and made blatant statements of unsubstantiated fact that supported his actions. He came across as being very sure of himself but overall ignorant of scientific fact.

Anne understood why Martha called Grant pig-headed and spent some time exploring his reasoning with him. She challenged his views, but he was able to defend his stance and she took note that he was still quite firm on his understanding.

"So, Grant, Brock is confused, Martha has been brainwashed and Mackenzie is opinionated, but they all seem to agree with each other. How does that make you feel?"

"I feel ganged up on that if I don't switch over to their way of thinking I'll lose my family. I don't know if I can change, this is who I am."

"Isn't that what you did to Brock, asked him to be something he isn't, or he loses his family?"

Grant heard her words and they connected in some small way in a part of his brain that caused him to stare at her as he digested her message. He sat there saying nothing.

Anne let him think and then broke the silence, "Our time is almost up, so I want you to think about all the things we talked about today. What we do know is your family is fractured and I want you to think about your role in that. Will you do this?"

"Yes, I will try."

"I have your appointments set up for every Saturday morning going forward at this time. I hope that is good for you."

"Yes, that works."

"Martha has arranged for payment, so I will see you next week."

*****

When he got home, Martha was taking biscuits out of the oven to have with the chicken soup she had made.

"Lunch is almost ready, wash up and I will have it on the table by the time you're back."

He returned to steaming bowls of soup and sat down.

Martha waited for him to offer some comment on his first session, but he took a biscuit and buttered it. He then proceeded to eat the soup and three more biscuits talking about the weather and then switched over to seeing a neighbour at the gas station, but nothing about his session.

Grant knew she wanted to know how the session had gone but said nothing. He waited for her to ask.

She didn't.

Chapter 21

It was four weeks to the day since Alice had moved into Caring Hearts Hospice. She went into a coma just before lunch and Brock was sitting next to her bed, holding her hand. She had awoken and he could barely make out what she was trying to say so he leaned in close. She locked her eyes to his and whispered "Honey, you have made my life complete. I love you!" Her eyes disconnected from his, drifted a little and slowly closed.

Brock panicked and responded to keep the conversation going. "Mammie, you mean the world to me. I love you so much!" As he finished the last word, he was happy to see that she opened her eyes for what was to be her last time, smiled, and gave a laboured wink before whispering, "I know." An intense energy flowed between them as they stared into each other's eyes until hers closed and it was gone. He felt like they had shared something so powerful that, in the coming years, he would never be able to find the words to adequately describe it.

He felt hunger pangs but didn't want to risk going out to get something to eat so he stayed and was determined to endure his hunger. Debbie, a fifty-something volunteer who Brock had gotten to know because of her bubbly personality, big compassionate heart, and caring way came to the door at twelve-thirty. "I thought you might be hungry; can I get you anything?"

"Thank you, I'm starving, but I was afraid to leave her. I would be good with anything."

Debbie suggested, "I can get you a bowl of corn chowder from the Soup Bar if you would like."

"That would be perfect." He pulled some money from his pocket and passed it to her. "Thank you."

She returned with a tray full of food and sat it down on Alice's table. "Enjoy. I will drop in every so often to see if you need anything more."

"Could I ask a favour?"

"Sure, what can I do for you?"

"I don't want her to be alone and I have to pee. Could you sit with her for a few minutes?"

"You go and don't worry; I won't leave until you return."

Brock was back in no time and all afternoon he sat and watched her, replaying her last words over and over in his mind. He wasn't acutely aware that he was gaining some small relief watching her chest rise and fall with each successive inhale. To him, it meant she was still with him. He had gotten to know the Nurse Manager, Marie, and found her to be very helpful. She popped in to see him when she heard Alice was in a coma. Brock made sure they stopped just outside the door so he could watch Alice's breathing. He asked Marie what he should expect to happen.

Marie had Alice's chart with her and as she spoke, she referred to the notes that the staff had made. "No one can predict when someone will die for certain, but there are signposts along the journey that tell of someone's dying and her coma is one of those signposts. She may wake from the coma, but her shallow breathing is another signpost, and my guess is that she won't wake, but I could be wrong. When the patient starts shallow breathing, we ask people to prepare themselves for their loved one's passing. It could be a matter of hours or days; it all depends on the will of the patient. Her pain management is working well, and we'll monitor for any signs of discomfort and continue to manage it. There is no reason for Alice to be in pain, so if you see anything, simply tell the staff and they will address it. Doctor O'Mally has prescribed everything we need to make sure her journey is as pain-free as possible. She can still hear so you can continue to talk with her if you want."

Brock listened and understood, only too clearly, "Is it alright if I stay with Alice overnight? I don't want her to be alone when she passes."

Marie nodded, "Certainly. We can have a cot brought in if you would like."

Brock had already thought about this. "Thank you, but I prefer the recliner that's right next to her bed."

Marie was used to people using the recliners, but some preferred the cots. "That's fine too. If you need anything let me know and when I'm not here, the staff on duty will be able to answer your questions or get answers for you."

Brock called Andrew and Gregory and told them about Alice and his decision to stay with her. He then called Matthew and explained things to him.

Matthew asked, "Is there anything I can bring you?"

"Thanks, but the guys are putting an overnight bag together and they are bringing me supper. You don't need to but if you want to come with them, I'm sure they wouldn't mind bringing you along."

"I will call them. You take care of yourself." Matthew's concern was evident in his voice. "I love you!"

"Don't worry, I'm fine. I just don't want Mammie to be alone when she passes." He wasn't sure if he had let any of the major anxiety he was feeling out in his conversation; he hoped he was hiding it well. "I love you too."

It was six-thirty when they arrived and after hugs from all of them, they settled down to talk. The guys brought Brock a container of pasta that he heated up in the Family Kitchen and brought it back to the room.

Brock ate his meal as he told them about his day, Alice's decline to the coma, and the conversation he had with Marie. "This pasta is delicious; is it a new recipe?"

Gregory beamed. "It's an old favourite from when Andrew and I first got together, and we haven't had it in years. I was going through some files on the computer and came across the recipe, so I decided to make it for supper."

Matthew's interest had peaked, "Now I have to taste it too."

Brock filled a forkful for him to eat.

Matthew savoured the mouthful, looked at Gregory and remarked, "OMG, it is amazing! Can I have the recipe?"

"Sure!" Gregory loved it when people enjoyed his food. "I will send it to your email tonight."

Andrew was watching Alice the whole time and he turned to get the others' attention. He made a few downward motions with his palms facing the floor to silently hush their conversation. He motioned for them to step outside the room. "When people are dying, many people believe they can still hear even though they are in a coma. I noticed Alice's breathing has become a lot slower in the half hour we have been here. I saw the same thing happen when my mom passed. I think she is on her way."

Brock's face scrunched up and tears flowed down his cheeks. "I need to get someone." He left them and went to the nursing station.

Andrew turned to Gregory, "I cannot leave Brock here by himself so I will stay when you have to leave. You go home and get some rest and you can replace me tomorrow if she hasn't passed by then. I don't think she will still be here, but you never know in these situations."

Brock returned with Marilyn, the nurse who just came on duty. She was talking as they walked. "I looked at her chart and was just about to check and see how she was doing." When they reached the room, she nodded to the other three, but spoke directly to Brock, "You can come in with me if you would like." They entered the room, and the others could see that Marilyn was taking Alice's vitals. She talked briefly and they both came out to the others. "It looks like it won't be long so if you have things to say to her, this is the time to do it. She can still hear you. I would suggest a calm tone of voice when you speak with her. I will check in every half hour or so, but if anything happens or you need something, press that button." She pointed to the button tied to the bed rail. She placed her hand on Brock's arm and comforted him with, "If you need me, I'm only minutes away." before she walked down to the nursing station.

Brock turned to go back in, but Matthew caught him by the shoulder and hauled him into a hug. "I'll be going, but if you want me here, I will stay. I just don't want to intrude."

Brock looked at him. "You wouldn't be intruding, but I'm okay, you go home; it could be a while. I'll text you if she dies."

Gregory hugged Brock, "Andrew will be staying with you while I go to get some rest. I will replace him in the morning if you are still here."

Brock released the hug. "That's okay, I'll be fine. She may not die today; nobody knows for sure. All of you need to go home and get your rest."

Andrew stepped in front of Brock, put his hands on both shoulders and looked him right in the eye. "Brock, the death of a loved one is the hardest thing we have to deal with in life and I'm not letting you go through this alone. I'm staying; no discussion."

Brock smiled, "Thank you. I really would appreciate not being alone."

Matthew and Gregory said their goodbyes and left. Brock and Andrew went into the room and each selected a chair, one on each side of Alice's bed.

Brock looked at Alice and her breathing seemed even lower. He looked around and picked up Alice's book on spirituality. He opened to the page he had stopped on earlier and began to read to her, in a slow, calm voice.

True to her word, Marilyn popped in every half hour and had been there five times since Andrew and Brock began their vigil. She had just come in for her sixth visit and took Alice's vitals. She turned to Brock slowly nodding while whispering, "Her vitals are becoming very weak; it could be soon." Before she left, she put her hand on his shoulder and gave it a squeeze.

Andrew spelled Brock in reading Alice's book. He had just finished an insightful piece when he lowered the book and whispered to Brock. "You never mentioned this side of Alice before. If this is her favourite book, I can understand the comfort she would get from these passages."

Brock nodded as he spoke and whispered his response, "If I had to use one word to describe who Mammie was, I would say spiritual would cover it so well. Some of my first memories of her are laced with life wisdom similar to what we have been reading. She was an amazingly well-read, compassionate, and insightful person. It was her wisdom that she shared with me that helped me put together the perspectives and views I have of this world and the people in it. I don't know if I'll ever again know someone as special as she is to me."

At that moment he glanced down to see her exhale. He waited for her to inhale, but time ticked on and he became more anxious. "Andrew, she isn't breathing!" He reached for the button and pressed it repeatedly. Just then, Alice inhaled.

Marilyn arrived within seconds and Brock explained. "I thought she stopped breathing, but after I had already pressed the button, she inhaled. Sorry, I guess I panicked."

Marilyn took her vitals. "She is still here, but she is well on her way. It won't be long now."

Brock held Alice's hand and watched her labour to inhale and exhale with long intervals in between breaths. He leaned close to Alice's ear and whispered, "I love you, Mammie." When he leaned back and watched, no inhale came. He started to shake, and Andrew went around the bed, bent over him and held him as he wept. He held Brock until his sobs subsided and he had collected himself. Brock reached over and pressed the button.

Marilyn came in and confirmed that Alice was gone. "You spend whatever time you need and when you're ready, we can call the funeral home." She left them alone. It was almost midnight.

Brock stood and, as he did, a new wave of grief washed over him. Andrew held him and let him sob.

Suddenly, Brock lifted his head off Andrew's shoulder with eyes wide open. "Do you feel that?"

Andrew hadn't noticed anything, but then he felt it. "I do." was all he could say.

They stood looking at Alice's still form as the room filled with an invisible substance, an energy like nothing they had ever experienced. It was palpable. The room was full, and the air moved with an invisible force, a presence of sorts. They were not afraid; they were in awe. They looked at each other and both basked in the feeling of knowing that Alice's soul was on the move. As fast as the room filled, it diminished and returned to normal although, from that day forward, neither Brock nor Andrew would be able to use that word again. Could they really know what *normal* was ever again?

They were with her for 30 minutes and Brock told the staff to call the funeral home. He had called Wade Jackson and informed him of Alice's death and after some reassurance that he was okay and didn't need him, he told Brock he would be in touch.

The funeral directors arrived. Andrew and Brock left Alice's room to join the ceremonial honour guard made up of staff and a few family members of other patients. All holding lighted candles, they lined both sides of the hallway to bid her farewell. They wheeled a gurney with Alice's body, draped in a home-made sunflower quilt out into the hallway. She passed through the two rows of lights before disappearing into the elevator. Brock was alone in his thoughts reviewing Alice's final words to him. His eyes watered, but he didn't weep, and Andrew quietly passed him a few tissues.

They collected Alice's things with the help of Marty, a Personal Support Worker, and when everything was packed up, Brock said his goodbyes before he and Andrew made their way to the car. They sat in the cold while Andrew warmed the car, and they reviewed all that had happened that evening. Brock reached over, squeezed Andrew's shoulder, and thanked him for staying with him.

Andrew responded, "There was no way I was going to leave you to face this on your own. In the short time we have known you, we have come to see you as part of our family; we love you."

Brock leaned over and hugged him. "Thank you. I do feel loved."

Andrew put the car in gear, "Let's go home."

Chapter 22

Brock arrived in the kitchen dressed in a dark blue suit and Gregory commented, "I didn't think it was possible for you to look even more handsome and there you go proving me wrong."

Andrew chimed in, "Nice suit. Alice was quite the planner to have purchased it and had it ready for you to wear to her funeral."

"Yes, Wade Jackson had it all set up like Mammie wanted. I'll be able to wear this to my graduation as well."

"We'll drive over together for ten o'clock, so you can have some private time with her ashes before the public starts arriving for ten-thirty in the chapel. They have one hour before the funeral at eleven-thirty. She was quite an efficient planner."

"Yes, after the funeral service there will be a luncheon right at the funeral home. From there, we'll have a private burial between one and two o'clock depending on the people who attend. With most of her friends gone and having no family, we're expecting a small crowd."

*****

They met Wade at the funeral parlour, and he took Brock down the hall while Matthew, Andrew, and Gregory followed them only so far and waited while they went into the chapel alone. Brock opened the doors about ten minutes later and asked them to come in. There was a nice picture of Alice on a table with her urn and an arrangement of her favourite flowers that Brock had purchased. Alice didn't want any flowers unless Brock wanted some and his were to be the only ones.

Ten-thirty arrived, and people started to trickle in; some neighbours, staff from businesses she had used, her caregivers Paula and Valerie, and Brock's mom, dad, and sister. This was the first time he had seen his parents together since he was kicked out. His dad froze when they spotted each other. Mackenzie walked away from them and hugged Brock. Martha started to step forward after Mackenzie, but Grant tugged on her arm. She broke free of his hold and hugged Brock. His father led his mother to seats well back from Brock's reserved seat in the front row. Matthew, Andrew, Gregory, and Mackenzie were seated there to support him.

There were no more than thirty people in the pews and the service was more spiritual than religious with Wade acting as the officiate. "I would like to call on Brock Matheson to say a few words."

Brock stood at the lectern and looked out over the small gathering. "Alice DesRoches was our next-door neighbour all of my life, but she was so much more to me; she was my 'Mammie' and I was her 'Honey'. I met her in her back garden one day when my mom had Mackenzie and me out in our back yard and I wandered over. That chance meeting was the start of a wonderful relationship. She taught me a lot about gardening, but more about life in general. She was a free spirit who didn't care what people thought and knew more about me, sometimes before I did, than most people. No matter what, she always accepted everything about me." At this point, he looked into the audience, found his father, stared him right in the eyes, and continued. "She never rejected me, no matter what I told her or more importantly, what she had already guessed about me. No matter what crisis I found myself in, she always welcomed me with open arms and was a wonderful source of love and support. If more people could embrace unconditional love like she did, the world would be a far better place." He saw his father's face turn his characteristic deep purplish red a sign that he was in a silent rage. Brock hoped he got his message across. He summed up, "I will miss you Mammie; life will never be the same." He lowered his head and dabbed his eyes before returning to his seat.

Mackenzie had more tissues at the ready and put her hand on his shoulder to comfort him.

Wade finished the service, announced that the burial would be private and invited everyone to the luncheon.

Brock told the others to go ahead and he would be there shortly as Wade asked him to stay behind to discuss something with him. They left, and in no time, Wade and Brock were the only ones in the chapel. The funeral director took Alice's urn, the flowers, and the picture and closed the doors for their privacy.

"As Alice's executor I need to meet with you to go over her wishes. Is tomorrow morning good for you?"

Brock thought about what he had planned for the next morning and responded, "Yes, that would be fine."

"What time would be good for me to come to your place? I only need an hour of your time at most, but we can take longer if you need."

"I'm up early so nine o'clock would work well for me. Do you know where I'm living?"

"Great, I will be at Mahogany Manor for nine. Alice gave me your new address when I visited her in Hospice. Let's not keep our guests waiting." Wade opened the door and turned left down the hall with Brock at his side.

When they got to the luncheon area, there were about twenty people milling around and Brock's parents were not among them. He was not surprised after he saw his father's reaction to his comments. Mackenzie had stayed and he started to make his way over to her. As he walked, people stopped him, gave him their condolences, and one person, who he didn't know, remarked, "That was a wonderful tribute you gave. Sorry for your loss."

He saw Stephen Wycott approaching with his hand extended to shake. "Your tribute to Alice was so heartfelt. She thought the world of you as well."

"Thank you. We had a very special relationship."

"I have some things that we need to discuss. I was wondering if you could come to my office tomorrow." He handed Brock a business card. "Here's my address."

"I'm meeting with Wade Jackson to discuss the will at nine and he says we wouldn't need more than an hour. Would eleven work? "

"Eleven works well. If you find you need more time with Wade, I have some flexibility with my schedule, just give me a call."

"Do I need to bring anything?" Brock inquired.

"No, I just need you. See you tomorrow." He turned and walked away.

Mackenzie tapped his shoulder. "How are you doing Brock?"

"I'm doing well. It's hard to believe she is gone. Where are Mom and Dad?"

"Where do you think they are? Dad took Mom's arm and led her out to the car. I think she would have stayed but didn't want to make a fuss in public. Your tribute had to make them think about their own behaviour. I especially liked the part about the unconditional love!"

The numbers dwindled quickly and before long it was just Andrew, Gregory, Matthew, and Mackenzie left, so Brock told the funeral director they were ready to go to the cemetery.

Wade was there already when they arrived and with everyone gathered around the small hole, read a few words that Alice had written. Her urn was placed in the grave in front of the headstone that contained her name and the names of her husband Benjamin "Benny" and their son Daniel 'Danny'. Brock knelt, bowed his head and whispered something to Alice. He then brought two fingers to his lips and kissed them before touching them to the urn. He let them linger for several seconds in quiet contemplation before lifting them off and standing. He took a flower from his arrangement and placed it on the urn. Just before it was lowered into the ground. He turned away from the grave and said goodbye to Wade and the funeral director before getting into the car with the others to go to '*the Manor*'.

During the drive home, Brock recounted the conversation he had with Wade about the will. "Wade is coming to see me tomorrow morning at nine to talk about Mammie's estate and her wishes. I guess I'm in her will. I also have an appointment with her financial manager at eleven o'clock. I have no idea why, but I guess I'll find out tomorrow."

Mackenzie got excited, "I wonder what she left you? She had no family so maybe you're her heir."

"I can't even imagine. She gave me that family heirloom watch already, so it will be interesting."

Chapter 23

Andrew, Gregory, and Brock were finishing their breakfast when the doorbell rang, and they all glanced at the clock. Andrew was the one to comment, "He's punctual, I have to give him that!"

Brock left the table and went to the front door. "Good morning, Wade, come in. Would you like a cup of coffee?"

Wade shook his head. "Thank you, but no, I'm fine."

"We're going up to the guest family room; it's a quiet place where we won't be disturbed." Brock took the lead and Wade followed.

They sat down and Wade pulled out some papers. "Alice was very well organized so her wishes will be simple to execute. As you know, she has no living family and she loved you very much. She saw you as a son and named you as the sole heir to her entire estate. The estate consists of her home, bank accounts with a total value of $5,762, a few small investments worth about $48,943 as of yesterday afternoon, and all of her personal effects."

Brock sat back in his chair and looked at Wade. He was the sole heir. "I'm flabbergasted. I had no idea I would be her heir."

Wade explained, "Alice discussed her will with me and she was very clear that you're her rightful heir. She thought it might be a lot for you to understand right away, but she made sure there was money enough to look after all of the house expenses for months and years to come."

"What do I need to do?"

"The estate isn't large enough to concern ourselves with probate so we can begin executing her wishes right away. The banking should be simple. The easiest way is for you to open accounts in your name and I can write you cheques to deposit. I can disperse some of the money, but I need to pay any bills and process her final income tax before I can disperse the final amounts to you and close the estate. For one this simple, it typically takes a little more than a year to accomplish everything. I will set up an appointment with her lawyer to legally transfer the house over to you within the week, but you can move in anytime; it is yours. Here are the keys to your house. Do you have any questions?"

Brock asked a few questions to clarify his understanding but there wasn't much else. "This is so new to me. Is there something I should be asking that I'm not?"

Wade shook his head, "No, this is a simple straight-forward estate. If you think of anything that I can help you with, please give me a call."

Brock thanked him and saw him out.

*****

After Wade left, Brock went to his room to try and digest all that had happened over the past month and the information Wade had just given him. It was a lot, but he now understood that Mammie wanted him to have everything. He looked at the keys and remembered her saying, '*my home is your home.*'. It meant so much for him to be loved.

He looked at his phone for the time. He still had to meet with Stephen Wycott at eleven o'clock.

Brock wondered what Stephen could want. His mind went around and around considering different scenarios but came up with nothing. He had no idea what they would be talking about, but it had something to do with her finances.

He entered the office at ten-fifty-five and Sylvia greeted him, "You are Brock Matheson; I recognize you from Alice DesRoches' funeral. I'm so sorry for your loss. Your tribute to her was wonderful. I have known her almost thirty years and she was always such a sweet lady.

"Thank you for saying that. She was pretty special to me."

"Stephen is expecting you and will be out in a moment, please have a seat."

Brock headed for the first chair on the left and picked up a MacLean's magazine to thumb through while he waited, but before he could take his seat, Stephen opened his door and invited him in.

He shook Brock's hand, "Come on in and have a seat."

Stephen brought out a thick file from his drawer and opened it saying, "I know Alice never mentioned this to you because she asked me not to contact you until after the funeral. She listed you as the beneficiary to most of her investment portfolio."

Brock was confused, "I met with Wade Jackson, her executor, this morning and he told me I was her heir and inherited everything, so wouldn't her investments be included in that?"

91

"No, because she listed a beneficiary, the investments aren't included in the estate. They go directly to the person listed and that is you. She thought very highly of you and loved you like a son. I looked forward to meeting you because of the high praise she used when she described you."

Brock let his words sink in, but he was incapable of processing what he thought this meant. "But…but.."

"Brock, I know this is a shock and I will explain everything. Before I do, Alice wanted you to read this letter first and this second one she gave me while in Caring Hearts which she wanted you to read after the first."

He saw his name written on the envelope in her handwriting. He took his time opening the first envelope trying to preserve this last piece of Mammie; she had touched this letter.

He slid it out and unfolded the top third.

'*Honey,*'

Seeing Mammie's special name for him, brought her sweet voice into his memory and he heard her saying it like she did thousands of times over his lifetime. It was enough to break his emotional control and he began sobbing.

Feeling Brock's raw, unguarded pain, Stephen went around the desk and put his hand on his shoulder to comfort him.

The sobs abruptly subsided. Brock was embarrassed with his reaction, "I'm so sorry you had to see that."

"Don't be. You and Alice shared a special relationship, and your reaction is testament to that. Do you feel up to reading the letter? We can do this another day if you want."

"As long as you do not mind some tears, I think I can do this; I have to do this. Mammie would want me to." He sat up straighter in his chair, steadied himself as he unfolded the rest of the letter, and began to read.

'*Honey,*

I hope you are doing well, and my demise hasn't been too hard on you. I love you more than anyone or anything in my life and I'm writing this because there are things I want you to know. I had told you about my family rejecting me and that they were killed in a car accident, but I didn't tell you that I was the sole heir to my parents' estate in 1936. I had grown up in privilege and my father was from a well-known family, so I inherited a lot of money.

Benny was a proud man and refused to use any of the money from a man who caused me so much heartbreak, so it sat invested all these years. When Benny died, I was comfortable in my life and didn't want for anything, so I left it invested without thinking of what would happen to it when I was gone.

That's until I was told I had terminal cancer and the answer was right in front of me. I have made you the beneficiary for the entire investment from my family. Stephen's firm has managed the family fortune long before I was born but for the past 79 years, they have managed it for me. Their advice helped me, and I encourage you to use his expertise to help manage your new fortune. You are a very responsible person and I have always been very proud of you. I was just a little older than you when I inherited it and I place no strings on this gift whatsoever; it's your money free and clear! I wish you nothing but the best in life and, if you stay true to who you are, I see a very fulfilling life for you. Please enjoy your life and use the money to make it wonderful; you deserve it!

With all my love,
Your Mammie

Brock tried to digest what he had just read when he remembered the second letter. He opened it and saw that it was also in her handwriting only shakier than in the first note. He read.

'Honey,

By now you have read my first note that told you of the fortune. You do not know how much yet, but Stephen will tell you shortly.

The reason I have added this second letter is from the 'What If' game we played at Caring Hearts. One of the 'what-ifs' asked you was 'what if you had money, what would you do?' and you impressed me with your answer; you didn't think of yourself like some people might have, you responded like the Brock I know and love. You thought of all the people who find themselves without a home and you would build them a safe place to go. That touched me deeply because both of our families chose to dismiss us from their lives. Now you have money. Have fun.

I love you more than I could believe possible!
Your Mammie'

Brock finished reading, but he continued looking at the letter and focused on the signature. He was in disbelief. She called it his fortune and when that thought entered his head he looked up to Stephen, "She says it's a fortune. How much money are we talking?"

"Alice always was the investor as Benny wanted nothing to do with her father's money and she was shrewd. My great-grandfather and then my grandfather were her father's investors and she remained with him until my father took over. When I took over, she was very active in the growth of the fortune which today is valued at $97,678,368.55."

Brock's eyes grew large and he swallowed hard before managing a question to verify what he thought he had heard. "Did you say ninety-seven million?"

"It's more than a half million over the ninety-seven million mark; "Ninety-seven million, six hundred-seventy-eight thousand, three-hundred-sixty-eight dollars and fifty-five cents to be exact."

"Wow!" was all Brock could say and then he sat there in silence staring at the floor when his shoulders started shaking and he broke out in sobs.

Stephen, again, went to Brock to comfort him. "I know this is a lot to take in, but Alice loved you so much she wouldn't want to cause you pain."

"Her death is more painful than this money. I would give every cent back if I could have her in my life again."

Brock calmed and Stephen went back to his seat. "Are you okay Brock?"

"Besides having my body go entirely numb I can't even tell you. I think I'm dumbfounded; I would never have guessed she had this kind of money and that she would leave it to me. Before today, if I got my paycheck of a few hundred dollars, I felt rich. I just can't grasp how much money this is."

Stephen looked at Brock, "I can't imagine anyone being able to completely grasp the enormity of this inheritance. Remember, she shrewdly invested and didn't touch a cent of her inheritance from her father's estate. It has been invested for almost eighty years."

"My head is going nuts thinking about what I should do next."

"You don't have to do anything right away. Give yourself time to let this sink in. You have just inherited a large fortune and I have seen mismanagement lay waste to fortunes of similar size in a small number of years. I would like to discuss having our firm continue to manage it for you. How do you feel about that?"

"No need for discussion. If she trusted you, I will too. You are hired."

"Thank you for trusting us with your business."

He was still in disbelief, but felt numbness starting to subside, "So, all that money is mine? If I wanted some, how do I go about getting it?"

"Yes, legally it's all yours. Anytime you want any, just let me know and I will get it for you. You could also have a regular income set up if you wanted. Think about it and we can talk. In the meantime, I need you to sign some paperwork to transfer the money over to you, but that isn't a huge issue. How soon will you want some money?"

"That second letter helps me understand where some of it will go. I'm going to build a shelter for homeless people in Mammie's honour. I do not want people to know I'm doing it so if you could manage the financial process, I will find a contractor and start the project. As for me, I need some time to digest all that has happened today. I understand there is money that she left in the bank accounts which will cover the running of the house for a bit, so I need to understand what running a house will cost. Once I do, then we can talk. In the meantime, you can go ahead with the transfer." Brock extracted a business card from his shirt pocket and passed it to Stephen, "Here is Wade Jackson's contact information. He is the executor and can provide you with whatever information you need."

"Alice had connected us, and I contacted him to get a copy of the death certificate so I can move ahead on this. I need you to sign these forms. As for managing the process of building the shelter, yes, we can fund the process with your money, and we will look after all the financials. I suggest you connect with a lawyer for the rest."

"Ok, I'll be contacting Mammie's lawyer and I'll let you know when the project will begin. I know it is a while, but I will keep in touch when I know what the projected costs will be." Brock went to work signing the many forms Stephen provided and when he finished, he asked, "Is that all you need from me?"

"I would like to meet with you in a few weeks but there is no rush. I want to discuss investment strategies, explain the composition of your portfolio, and determine what your financial goals are going forward besides building the shelter."

"I did well in economics in school, but I never considered I would have an investment portfolio this early in my life. I'm a quick learner, but you will need to be patient with me. If I don't contact you, call me in a month and we can set a date for the meeting."

"Thank you, Brock, I look forward to managing your portfolio. If there is anything that we can do for you, please do not hesitate to call."

Brock shook Stephen's hand and left the office in a stupor. He made it back to 'the Manor' without really knowing how he got there, but the hollow thud of his feet on the front stairs awoke him to the reality that still seemed quite surreal.

Chapter 24

Brock entered the front hall and called out for Andrew and Gregory. They came from different parts of the house and met him in the front hallway. Gregory hugged him, "What's wrong; you look like you've seen a ghost?"

Andrew hugged him and when Brock started sobbing again, he led him into the living room and sat him on the sofa. "Don't worry guys, everything is more than fine, but I need to tell you what has happened. I also want Mackenzie to hear this, so I just texted her and she can be here in 15 minutes. I would like to have all three of you together when we talk. What I can tell you is that I've spent most of the day in tears."

Gregory offered a suggestion, "That gives us enough time to put some refreshments together, that is, if we all help. I'm in suspense and I don't want anyone to start talking without me."

They worked together talking about nothing of substance, but everyone's mind was somewhere else. They put together a platter of pieces of fruit, slices of cheese and an assortment of crackers. Drinks were poured and Andrew went searching for napkins when Mackenzie bounded up the stairs to the verandah. Brock let her in, gave her a big hug as did Gregory and Andrew. "Gee Bro, you look like shit and I mean that in the nicest way!"

They all laughed and went to gather the platter, napkins, and drinks and went to the private living space without saying another word. They took their seats and Brock noticed they always sat in the same spot they did any time they needed to talk about something, but this time Mackenzie filled a fourth seat. All eyes were on Brock.

When he didn't immediately start, Andrew decided he would break the tension. "So, Brock what's up?"

He looked at them and started. "I met with Mammie's executor this morning and learned she listed me as the sole heir to her estate, so I own her home, all of her furnishings and household goods, some investments, and her bank accounts."

Andrew assessed what Brock had said. "She had said she didn't have any family when she gave you that watch which was a family heirloom. She must have seen you as her family so I can understand her doing that."

Mackenzie smiled a huge smile, "Good for you. You now have your own home, and no one can kick you out. Did she leave you enough money to afford the place?"

"Yes, I'll be able to afford it, but that isn't all of it. I don't even know how to digest all of this, but I met with her investment manager and she listed me as beneficiary on her investments. She wrote me these letters which I had to read before I would hear what the investments were worth." He took the letters out of his shirt pocket and passed the first one to Gregory as he was in the middle. I would like all of you to read it before I give you the second." Andrew and Mackenzie huddled in so they all could read it together. When they finished, they each looked up in stunned silence. He then gave them the second letter which they read with eager anticipation.

Andrew whistled, "Family fortune, who knew?"

"Wow, just wow! This is something right out of a mystery novel." Mackenzie exclaimed as she reread the letter. "Are you rich Bro?"

Brock responded, "I am. I still think I'm dreaming, but I couldn't possibly dream this because Mammie was Mammie and I never had an inkling that she had any money. In all the years I have known her, she never let on, so it was a huge shock."

Andrew asked what was on all their minds. "Do you mind if we ask how much she left you. If you aren't comfortable telling us, do not feel pressured in any way. We're just being nosey."

"You three are the only ones I'll tell. I ask that you do not share this with anyone else. I need you to swear?"

They wanted to hear so badly that there was resounding, "I swear." from all three.

"Thank you, I don't mean to insult you, but this is very scary for me. As of today,........." He took another page out of his pocket, unfolded it and continued, "...... as of today, my investment portfolio is worth $97,678,368.55!"

All three fell back into their chairs, like dominoes, after being on the edge of their seats prior to his announcement. They each were running the figure over in their minds when Mackenzie broke the spell. "You did say ninety-seven million, didn't you?"

"I actually said ninety-seven million, six-hundred-seventy-eight thousand, three-hundred-sixty-eight dollars and fifty-five cents." Brock ended with a huge, nervous smile on his face.

Mackenzie summed up what was racing through her mind. "You're rich! Hell, I would have said you were rich if you had one ninety-seventh of that amount. You're super rich! This must be the most exciting news I have ever heard in my life and I can't tell anyone! Bummer! Thanks Bro!"

"All the way home from the investments manager I thought about those people who have to hire guards because of kidnapping or extortion. This kind of money can bring out the worst in people. The more I thought, the more I realized Mammie had this fortune and no one bothered her because she never told anyone. That will be my strategy going forward at least until I figure all of this out. I really want to live a simple, happy life. I hope you understand."

Andrew and Gregory were deep in thought about what this all meant and were sorting things out in their heads about Brock not working there anymore. "Will you build the shelter she talked about in her second letter?"

Brock addressed Andrew and Gregory looking from one to the other. "About the shelter, yes, I want to build it and I would like to hire you both to be the project managers or general contractors or whatever you call it."

"You want us to do the planning and execution of the project from thought to reality, including all the logistics like land selection and purchase, building design, construction, staffing, and operation?"

"Yes, and I expect there will be other things we're not thinking of at this moment, but I basically want you to act as if you own this. I don't want anyone to know I'm involved and if you would manage the project, I can be involved, but invisible. My investment firm will manage the finances and I'll contact the lawyer to handle all the legalities, but you guys would do the rest. I pay well. What do you say?"

"This is a dream come true! We say yes." Andrew then remembered to include Gregory. "Am I right Gregory?"

"As always, I support you! This will be exciting."

Brock was happy they would do it. "We can work out the details some other day. This is almost too much to take in for one day."

Mackenzie thought about something and perked up, "Will you tell Matthew?"

"I don't see any reason for him knowing at this time. Not that I don't trust him, but it's information no one really needs to know. I will be sharing that I inherited her estate, but I don't have to go into all the details. I have decided I'll buy a modest car and moving into Mammie's house, but that will be the extent of the changes people will see. I still need to graduate and go to university, so I don't want any more attention than I get now and sometimes that can be overwhelming. I guess I'm going into another closet, of sorts, again."

Gregory agreed and joked a bit about what he said. "It definitely is a closet, of sorts, but what a fabulous closet that would be!"

"I need everything in my life to look the way it has been to everyone else, but we four will know better. I plan on keeping this job for a while if that's okay with you two." He said looking at Andrew and Gregory.

"Phew! I was being totally selfish when you told us and I went right to losing the best employee we ever had, but if you want to stay, we would love to have you! Since we have taken on another big job, we'll need you more than ever! Your conditions have changed a great deal, so if, in the future, you decide to leave, we would understand." Andrew assured him.

"Wade said I can move into Mammie's home anytime. I know there are things I need to do before I move in. I'll look after getting things done and then make my move. He looked at Andrew and Gregory, "Thank you for providing me with a safe sanctuary; I love you guys so much for all you have done for me and I will pay it forward with the building of the shelter. I want to call it the Alice DesRoches Homeless Shelter."

"What a wonderful way to honour her!' Mackenzie liked the idea that Brock would be living right next door, but realized, "Will living at Mammie's be too close to Dad for you?"

"After I left Stephen, I thought about what that would be like and where I'm now self-sufficient, I think it would be good for him to see I'm not suffering under his punishment. I can hardly wait till the first snowstorm when we shovel our driveways at the same time. There has to be a wicked streak in me because I'm relishing the thought way too much. Maybe I will be moving my boyfriend in with me sometime; who knows?"

Chapter 25

Brock went car shopping with Mackenzie and settled on an understated gray coloured Hyundai Elantra, a small economical car with good safety ratings. He negotiated the best deal, signed all the papers, and made a cash down payment. He used some of the money Mammie had left him in her will and had the bank certify the cheque, so he was able to pick up his car by noon the next day.

With Mackenzie's help, he determined when he could go to Mammie's house and not run into his parents. He wanted to be moved in before they found out.

He hired Paula to help him clear out things that he didn't want or need and one morning Paula told him about her inheritance. "When Alice's investment manager called and wanted to see me, I didn't have a clue why. I went to his office and there was a letter she wrote to me that I needed to read; it broke me up. What a dear soul she was. I have known her for more than twenty years, but I never knew she had that kind of money. I thought she was comfortable, but she left me a substantial amount."

Brock let her talk without saying anything about his inheritance. "She was a sweet old lady who kept her business to herself. It was a surprise to me too."

Just after lunch, Paula let more information out. "I inherited enough so I will never have to work again, so I will be giving up all my cleaning jobs. I'm doing this cleaning for Mammie because she would have wanted me to help you. She thought the world of you. In my letter, she said she saw me as the daughter she never had."

"What a wonderful remembrance she left you with? More than the money, the knowledge that she thought of you like that must warm your heart." Brock replied, still keeping things vague.

Paula responded, "It does, but leaving me the half million will be something that will help my family even after I'm gone."

"True, it must take a huge weight off your shoulders to have that nest egg."

The day was waning, and they had accomplished a lot, enough so Brock felt comfortable he could move in. They had put the final bags of garbage together and he texted Mackenzie to see if the coast was clear. He needed to put the garbage out, but before she could answer, his mother drove into the yard. He watched from behind a curtain as she looked at his car and then at the house before going in. When she did, he ran the final garbage bags to the curb. He paid Paula, said goodbye, wishing her well, locked the house up and drove to '*the Manor*' where he met Matthew.

They had supper with the guys, shared stories of what happened that day, and then packed up Brock's things. Everything went into a duffle bag, four boxes, and five garbage bags. They took everything down and loaded the car and waited until they heard from Mackenzie for her all clear.

Soon Mackenzie texted, 'Both parents are watching a ninety-minute special on TV about one of their favourite shows. It will be over at ten-thirty.'

This meant they had about an hour. Operation move-in was on! They drove over and parked right next to his dad's car. Brock unlocked the back door while Matthew started lugging things over. Brock took the things into the kitchen that Matthew had deposited by the door before going to the car for more. The car was emptied in no time and the two went to work unpacking and organizing where everything went.

Matthew went around the house making sure the curtains were closed before turning any lights on. He checked that the doors were locked and that the outside lights were off, so no one would think about visiting. He had Brock to himself for an hour before his curfew. He went back to the master bedroom where Brock was putting the final things away. "What does it feel like to be in your own place?"

Brock put his arms around him and hugged him whispering, "I still don't believe everything that has happened, and I will sleep in my own place for the first time tonight. Are you staying a while?"

"Do you want me to stay?" Matthew almost purred hoping for the answer he wanted to hear.

"What do you think?" he said just before his lips were busied on Matthew's. He kissed him with tenderness and planted small kisses down the side of his neck. Matthew shivered as the sensations took over his senses. Brock started undoing the buttons of Matthew's shirt and slid his hands along the warm flesh of his chest and bent down to kiss his nipple. This drove Matthew crazy with lust and he grabbed Brock's shirt and didn't care how it came undone. The shirt was off in seconds flat and his fingertips were gliding to all the areas he had discovered on Brock that caused him to moan. Brock wanted more and the clothing was, plain and simple, not needed. He undid Matthew's belt and jeans and slid his hands along his waist until they were in his briefs. With one smooth downward sweep, everything was at his ankles. Matthew bent over to dislodge the entanglement while Brock removed his clothes and was nude when Matthew stood up. They caressed and fell onto the bed. Their lovemaking was unrushed, and they explored new sensations with a whole new sense of freedom.

Chapter 26

Grant arrived in the kitchen to find Martha making breakfast. "Did you notice the gray car in Mrs. DesRoches' driveway? Did the house sell? Is there a new owner?"

Grant was going to therapy every week and he seemed less rigid, but she hadn't witnessed any big changes. Martha resumed her role as homemaker and handed him his plate, "I made scrambled eggs the way you like them." They moved to the table and took a seat. "I saw the car yesterday and I thought it might have belonged to a cleaner or someone dealing with the estate, but it's there this morning, so it might be the new owners."

"It wasn't on real estate that I know of, so someone either bought it from the estate or inherited it." Grant surmised.

Martha was quietly thinking and then announced. "If it's still there when I get home from work, I'll go over and introduce myself."

They continued talking and heard Mackenzie's footsteps coming down the stairs.

She entered the kitchen dressed for school. "Good morning!" She saw the eggs in the frying pan, popped some bread into the toaster and leaned up against the counter facing her parents. "What's new?"

Her father was the first to answer. "It looks like someone moved into Mrs. DesRoches' house. They have a gray car. Have you met them yet?"

"As a matter of fact, I know the new owner really well." She replied knowing the next little while was going to be interesting and she was looking forward to it!

Her mother asked, "Who is it?"

Mackenzie was evasive on purpose. "Someone you have known for awhile but have lost touch with. I don't think they are in your life anymore, so of course, you wouldn't know."

Grant pressed, "Who are they? What is their name?"

Mackenzie hesitated and then laid it out for them to get the full impact. "To honour your request that I not mention his name in family discussions I'll use his relationship to me; my brother is the new owner." She watched as the realization swept over both faces at the same time.

Grant was trying to sort it out. "Brock is the new owner? How can that be?"

"Yes, he is. Are we playing with new rules now where you can use his name, but I can't? Doesn't seem fair to me, but then again, I have never agreed with your decision from the start when you disowned him and kicked him out on his birthday." She got the whole statement out without being stopped and it felt good. It felt really good and now it lay in the air like thick, discoloured smog. She watched as her father's face began to distort ready to volley some edict at her, but it was pre-empted when her mother spoke.

"Did Mrs. DesRoches list Brock as an heir? Is that how he owns it?"

Her mother's face was portraying something Mackenzie was unable to define; something she couldn't remember seeing before. "Seeing that you both are using my brother's name, I will as well. "Yes, Mrs. DesRoches listed Brock as her sole heir. She loved him like her own son and when he came out to her, she embraced him, oh yes, and then gave him everything. He now owns her house, and he bought that gray car for cash last week. He is independent now, so your punishment for him being who he naturally is, isn't going to be very effective now, is it? He doesn't need this family; of course, he is '*dead to you*', isn't that how you so eloquently put it Dad? He wants his family, but you don't want him; you would rather he was dead. I find the whole thing very sad."

"Now missy, don't use that tone on us, we're your parents!" Her father admonished.

"You are also Brock's parent so start acting like one instead of some red-necked thug who is afraid that if anyone found out you had a gay son; they would question your manliness. Mom is getting it together, so you need to get your priorities right! When you have a child, you love that child no matter what; you don't get to pick and choose. I can't sit back and be okay with your decisions to exclude Brock from our family. Thank goodness he has Andrew and Gregory in his life."

"Don't start with those perverts. They are the reason he thinks he's gay."

"Really, you really believe that? That type of thinking is just pure ignorance and went out with your 8-track tapes; become informed and move into this century. Those perverts, as you call them, are more his parents than you are right now. They provide him with love, support and guidance, something you as parents have decided to withhold like you would withhold candy from a child until they stop misbehaving. He's not a child and he isn't misbehaving; he's gay not because he chose it, but because he was born that way. He couldn't choose gay any more than he could choose his eye colour, but you think it's okay to have blue

104

eyes because you have them. You need to get over yourself."

Although Martha agreed with Mackenzie, she couldn't condone rudeness. "Don't talk to your father like that. We brought you up to respect your parents."

"Well, I do not respect you right now. What are you going to do, kick me out too? I'll just move in with Brock, he loves me!" She sees her dad is about to interrupt her. "Don't you dare try to shut me up. You have been doing it my whole life and I'm fed up with that. I have something to say and it's about time you listened. All my life, you have brought me up and encouraged me to stand up for the downtrodden. Well, Brock is now the downtrodden and who put him there? You did. Mom has been going to Pflag meetings and making an effort to educate herself. Why are you not attending with her? No matter how long you disown Brock and no matter how loud you proclaim he is dead to you, isn't going to make him straight. If you can't get anything else through that head of yours, get this; you can't change gay. The only thing you can change is your ignorant attitude. The cure for ignorance is education. Become the father you always should have been. It isn't too late."

Grant glared at Mackenzie through her entire rant and his face went his normal deep shade of red it goes when he is upset but with purple splotches this time. "Are you done, missy?"

She holds his stare without flinching. "Did you hear any of what I said?"

"I'm not sure what you think you said, but I do know I've heard enough from you. I'm going to work." He got up and tromped out of the kitchen, grabbed his coat, and slammed the door when he left.

"Now you've done it!" Her mom lamented.

"I can only hope so. Something has to reach him." Mackenzie was still vibrating from being on her soapbox and felt a bit victorious at being able to stand up to her dad and get her full message out. That was a first.

Her mother looked at her in wonder as if seeing her for the first time. "You know he is going to the next meeting, I told you that. Aren't you afraid of him?"

"What can he really do to me? He isn't one to use physical violence. He uses his force in voice and words and I have decided they don't scare me anymore. I have adopted a new attitude. I look at 'what is the worst that can happen?' and prepare for that. I knew this was coming this morning. Brock and I are tight, and I know everything about his life. I helped him buy his car, in fact, I borrowed Dad's car to take him around. I helped him know when you and Dad were here, so he wouldn't run into you. I knew he was moving in last night because I told him you both were engrossed in your television show. We talked about this morning and how you both would be inquisitive about the car and that you would ask me. This is kind of a game for us because we cannot believe you both just don't get it. You're moving forward, but Dad is slower to change. When I asked myself, what is the worst that could happen, I would get kicked out and I do not have any problem with that. If Dad is threatened with the truth, I would rather be in a place of unconditional love and that's with Brock."

"We love you unconditionally."

"I know you really believe that Mom but saying it doesn't make it so. There seemed to be conditions on loving Brock."

"But that's changing for me and I am hoping your father will see his way out of his ignorance soon. I want my family back."

"You can have your family back as soon as you and Dad can love unconditionally. You must do more than say it. You have to live it in everything you do as a parent."

Chapter 27

All four Mathesons attended the April Pflag meeting and Grant watched as Andrew started the meeting and people introduced themselves. He listened and wondered what he should say. His turn came and he offered, "My name is Grant and I'm Brock's father." and thought *'that's enough for now'*. If someone had told him a month ago when he started his weekly therapy sessions that he would feel almost comfortable coming to this meeting tonight, he would have said they were crazy, but he surprised himself with the change in his attitude. His therapist was good like Martha had said and she was able to get him to see things in his behaviour without him feeling judged. He had progressed to knowing he was coming to Pflag for the good of his family.

Andrew gathered topics for discussion and determined what order they would be discussed. "Let's get the discussion going with coming out. Who would like to start?"

Brock saw hesitation hang over the group and he didn't want to miss this opportunity, so he jumped in. "I think the majority of people don't understand the fear that keeps a person in the closet. The fear that you will be rejected by your family and friends, that you will be ostracised by others in group settings, that you could lose out on opportunities, lose your job, your apartment or any number of things straight people don't even have to consider, all because you are gay. We fear the unknown outcome of the coming out process especially coming out to someone who judges gay as unacceptable. If people are open-minded and informed, coming out can be quite positive and freeing, but if people are close-minded and uninformed, coming out can be disastrous and completely outside of your control. Not knowing which result you will get makes the fear very real and it can be quite debilitating; rules your life, steals your freedom, forces you to be dishonest, and keeps others from knowing who you really are.

I can remember feeling I was different at an early age but didn't know it was called gay. I initially wondered what I was feeling and, when I started putting it together that I could be gay, my fear started to grow as I watched my dad calling the gay people on TV negative names. No one wants to be called those names and I started hiding things. I wasn't being honest about what I was feeling and thinking so no one would guess, especially my dad. I am his only son and I soon learned how he wanted me to act. I did what he wanted, so I would have him in my life. All along I wanted him to love me, not call me those names, so that is when, I believe, I put myself in the closet. Coming out erases a lot of that fear, but it isn't done once and it's over; coming out is a continual process."

Jack, a teen boy new to Pflag asked, "You say it's a continual process, but I thought once you came out, everyone would know. I'm not out to my family because I'm afraid they will disown me, but once you come out, what more is there?"

"To help understand, I need to ask if you're out to anyone in your life."

"Just a few friends, that's all."

"Then you've started the process of coming out. As you come out to more people, you will be continuing the process. You may think the coming-out process is done when you believe being gay is a non-issue, but when that old fear of rejection rears its ugly head from time to time, it puts you back in that closet until you decide not to give in to that fear.

There may be a time when you may want to be considered for opportunities, whether it be a job, an apartment, or whatever and the person who has the power of refusal over who is chosen is bigoted. You might fear that you wouldn't be considered if they found out you were gay. That's the power that fear has over us; we find ourselves compromising our integrity to play the game.

Personally, I find that I still have a fear of rejection at school; about losing opportunitie in the sports I play, how people will treat me, whether friends will reject me or treat me differently, all because I am gay. I feel I am really at the start of my coming-out process. Ther are people like the guys on my sports team, close friends from earlier grades, and some cousin who I want to know I am gay, but I haven't told yet. There are also some people I don't wan to tell because I don't believe they need to know, or I trust them. The trouble is that you hav no control over who will tell someone else that you are gay. It is a trust thing and always a balancing act until you don't care who knows. That is when you are truly out."

Grant watched and listened to his son and was impressed with how articulate he was. He heard and understood what he was saying for maybe the first time in his life. He drew some parallels with his life as he digested Brock's words. He decided he would talk with his therapist about them at his session in the morning. He couldn't believe it, but over the four sessions he had had, he moved from dreading them to looking forward to them. He liked th way Anne never judged him but asked him questions that challenged him to explore his thinking. He always felt respected, certainly not belittled like when Mackenzie confronted him at the house. That only served to get his back up although he had to admit he would find himself going over, in his mind, what she had said. He zoned back into the meeting but remained silent.

Breanne piped up, "Another aspect we have to consider is the visibility of your issue. Being transgender and going from male to female wasn't something I could hide for long. In the early part of my transition, I could hide some of the details and have people wonder why a guy would have dangling earrings or longer hair, but at some point, my transition was totally visible, so I had to come out on a grand scale. Brock, you can be invisible, no one could guess because you don't fit the usual stereotype, so you have the option of telling people on your own timeline. I do know that each of us have to decide on when to come out and how, but that's our decision. I could have chosen not to expose parts of my transition, but I did so because it was right for me."

Martha offers her insights, "I would like to explore the fear that Brock mentioned. I suspect we all have fears of being rejected or negatively judged. I'm seeing a therapist and haven't mentioned it to anyone until I mentioned it to my husband who was very surprised. I suppose I was in a closet from which I have since broken free. I don't know if it's the same and I certainly do not want to belittle the LGBT closet, but I'm thinking a closet is a closet no matter what your issue."

Mary joined in, "I agree with you that we can have fear about many issues. I find when I fear something, it all comes back to, will people still respect me, like me, involve me, or whatever if they knew about my issue. Will I belong? It takes me a long while to trust before I can share with some people."

Brock responded, "Even when I determine that I can trust someone will be able to handle my issue and not treat me differently, they can still disappoint me. If that happens, it can cause me to not open up so quickly another time. What I try to remember is that the most important person who needs to accept me is me. If someone has a struggle with me, that is their struggle, and I don't need to take it on. The most important thing I have realized is that I am responsible for my well-being, not anyone else's well-being. I say that, knowing a big part of me is about helping the underdog when they cannot help themselves and that can become a balancing act."

Martha nods and speaks up, "It makes me happy to hear you say that at your young age. It took me many years of taking on others' struggles and, only recently, did I come to that realization. I am proud of who you are Brock."

Grant digested what Martha said and thought about what he was feeling. '*Martha said that so easily and I choke just thinking of saying something like that. I am proud of Brock too, for many reasons, but I have never told him. Why can't I be as open as Martha? I guess I have lots to talk to Anne about tomorrow.'*

Chapter 28

Brock walked into the kitchen where Andrew and Gregory were preparing breakfast for their guests. "It looks like we have 10 for breakfast. Would you like me to finish setting the table?"

Andrew slapped his forehead, "That's my fault. I needed some dishes but got waylaid talking about the meeting last night and forgot all about what I needed. Yes, please finish it. When you are done, I want to get your take on what happened last night."

"Okay, I'll be just a few minutes."

Brock returned minutes later. "One couple is seated, and another had taken luggage to their car so I think we can start."

The breakfast was in full swing with the ten guests for about fifteen minutes, before things slowed down and all three returned to the kitchen. Gregory addressed Brock, "So, how do you feel about last night's meeting?"

"I guess I have mixed feelings. First of all, Dad was there so that was better than I thought. Secondly, since he was there, I was hoping for a bit more participation but that didn't happen."

"Your mom has stepped up to the plate. Did she really give your Dad the ultimatum she told us about last month?"

"I spoke with her a few days after the meeting and she said she laid it out plain and clear that their marriage was done if he didn't go to the Pflag meetings. Not only that, she also added that he had to go to a therapist as well and he has been through four sessions. When she told me, I was more than a bit surprised because sometimes Mom is all talk and no action, falling into subservience around him. This time she was dead serious. I guess an ultimatum can work if the stakes are high enough."

Gregory was listening intently and asked, "Did you know he was in therapy?"

"Not until Mom told me last night. Mackenzie knew but, for some reason, didn't feel it was important enough to tell me. Maybe she didn't want to raise my expectations. My dad and therapy are just not words I would ever have expected to hear together, let alone say. He goes every Saturday morning so I would say he is there as we speak."

"I would love to be a fly on the wall in those sessions!" Andrew said with a thoughtful look in his eyes.

*****

Brock, Gregory, and Andrew returned to 'the Manor' chatting about what they had just done at the lawyers' office. They went into the kitchen and busied themselves getting some lunch options out of the fridge and setting up a combination of foods on the table before sitting down.

Brock took some crackers and was cutting some cheese when he spoke. "Thank you, guys, again, for supporting me through this legal stuff for Mammie's homeless shelter. I never would have been able to understand all that we discussed. I never thought about it being run by a Board of Directors and registering it as a charity, but I understand the wisdom in that setup. I'll be able to still be behind the scenes but not be in the limelight. I could easily be a board member."

Andrew responded, "Yes, you could. We covered everything the lawyer felt needed to be set up and I think we will be ready to find a property for the shelter and as soon as he registers the name, we can go ahead with the purchase. Gregory and I have been driving around looking at all the possibilities, but we haven't narrowed anything down yet."

"Do you think you will find an old building somewhere that would work, or do we need to look at building from scratch?"

"There are pros and cons to both options. We will all know better when we have something to look at." Gregory added as he brought some glasses of their special lemonade to the table. "I am eager to actually get started!"

"Before we get too excited, we need to create the guidelines that will help us find the right property." Andrew offered.

Brock looked perplexed. "What guidelines are you thinking?"

Andrew continued, "Things like the services we will be offering, the number of people we want to house, what the best location for the shelter would be, what programs we would need to consider and what space in the shelter is needed to support those programs, and I'm sure there are other things that we just don't know about yet. Maybe we should visit some existing shelters and see what we could learn from them."

Brock thought about all the different facets to this project and asked, "I am glad you're managing this project. When I asked you to do this did you expect it to include this?"

"We have learned that when we take a project on that we are passionate about; we do anything and everything."

*****

Andrew introduced his list logic, "A lot of the preliminary work needs to be done and heading the list is property selection. What we decide to buy will dictate what we do next, either renovate or build from scratch. We contacted the real estate agent we have used in the past and let her know what we were looking for. She called yesterday and is coming by this afternoon with the properties that she believes will fit the bill. You can be part of that meeting if you want. We know you want to be involved in the background, but this is face-to-face with our agent, Kim Saunders. Your call."

Brock thought about the meeting, "I think I'll attend but I want you two to narrow the selection to the guidelines we set out after we visited the other shelters. If we could do this after the agent leaves, we can bring out the pros and cons without her questioning why I'm so involved. Once we decide, we can have her set up appointments in which I would also like to be included."

"She is used to us bringing people along when we look at a property so I don't think she will think anything of it. The thing we all have going for us is that you will be perceived as being too young to really be involved in this project. Your desire to be in the background will not be an issue." Gregory added.

*****

Kim Saunders arrived on time and they introduced Brock as the B&B manager. They sat at the dining room table so they would have lots of room to spread things out. She brought out a stack of property listing information, "I have found six buildings and four vacant lots I believe meet the criteria set out in your guidelines." She brought out copies and passed them around. "I didn't know if you would have your guidelines handy so I thought I would bring them. Now, I have prioritized them in the order of strongest fit, and I will explain as I present each one." She went to work telling them how each property connected with the guidelines and the potential that she saw. As each one was explained, they discussed the pros and cons that each property presented. There were definite options, and the agent made a list of the properties the guys wanted to visit. After she was done, she asked if they had anything they needed to add.

Gregory responded with, "Kim, I congratulate you on the work you have done. Our next step will be to look at the five properties we selected so far and tonight we will review all the information on the properties again and let you know if we want to view any others. See if you can set up viewings for tomorrow after 1:00 so we can get the B&B work sorted out in the morning."

Kim gathered up her things and put them in her big leather bag. "I will let you know. Thank you, guys; it is always great doing business with you." She shook hands all round and left.

"I'm really impressed with Kim; she was so thorough in rating each property against our guidelines! I think we will be choosing one of the options she presented." Brock showed excitement as he spoke.

Andrew cautioned, "Don't get your expectations too high. None of the properties Kim presented were hers so they may sound wonderful according to the listing information, but we have learned that sometimes a listing agent can use some kind of artistic license when writing up a property. We try to hold our excitement down until we actually view a property."

*****

Brock, Andrew, and Gregory arrived back at the B&B and Gregory suggested, "Let's go to the kitchen and talk about what we saw today before any of the guests arrive."

They laid out the real estate information and sorted it into high-potential properties and non-potential. It took a few minutes but, for the most part, they agreed on the properties that had potential.

Brock summed up the situation, "So, we have cast aside 5 of the 8 properties and we have one building we would need to renovate and two vacant lots for a new build. Let's talk about the pros and cons of renovating a building versus building from scratch."

"In any renovation you may not know all of the challenges that the building presents until you are already into the job. For example, when we renovated this house, 6 feet of the back corners on both sides were completely rotted out and the building was being held up by the boards. We had never considered that situation, but it had to be fixed. It wasn't a big deal but sometimes the issue could be. One of the biggest cons for me is the unknown." Andrew offered.

Gregory added, "Another con of renovating is that you need to work within existing parameters of the building and that can cause us to have to compromise on something we want."

They continued discussing the pros and cons and came to a realization. Brock was the one to speak it, "To me, it looks like we've narrowed it down quite well and it sounds like we are talking about a new build. Would you say I'm reading this correctly?"

Andrew agreed, "I think you summed that up quite nicely and it looks like the large vacant lot on Broad Street is our site. I think a new build will give us a chance to have everything we want; we now need to involve the architect. What do you think Gregory?"

"I am with you both. That lot is zoned for our project and it gives us room for expansion down the road if we want."

Andrew explained, "Okay, next step is to get the architect designing the shelter. I will set up a meeting with Julia Broadview to bring her on board. She does amazing work."

Brock shook his head, "I'm excited about getting the project going and I know I'm going to struggle not being involved. If I'm going to be in the background, I know I need to let you guys run with it. If I'm too involved, people might start asking questions, so I'm relying on you to let me know if that happens."

"We will have you involved at whatever level you want to be but if things get questionable, we will alert you. We know how exciting this can be and we will take no offense if you want to be more involved." Gregory assured him.

Chapter 29

Grant walked into his therapy session with such a sense of purpose that Anne was excited to hear what was on his mind. After he took his seat she asked, "So Grant, when you were here last week you had a Pflag meeting to attend last night. Did you go?"

"Yes, I went. I didn't want to go, and I hesitated as long as I could, but Martha wouldn't let me off the hook." He told her about his introduction and that he didn't say anything after that. He filled her in on what Brock said.

"First, why didn't you say anything after the introduction?"

Grant looked a little smug, "Well, if I have to tell the truth, I was staging a small protest. Martha said I had to go to the meeting but never said anything about participating so I didn't say anything. In the middle of my silent protest, I was caught off-guard. I never expected to get anything out of the meetings, but Brock spoke, and he said things I never allowed myself to think let alone say out loud. I became confused because he was saying things that I could never say. I was impressed with how articulate he was."

"What impressed you?"

"He was so comfortable talking about things I never could."

"Why do you say that?"

"While he spoke, I listened, really listened and realized he was talking about feelings that I have had. Even though he was talking about being gay, many of the feelings he brought out were about relationships, not gay feelings but life feelings. The fear he talked about is similar to fears I have had but I would never be able to talk about them like he did. I guess I never analyzed the fears and just accepted them as something that held me back without really knowing why."

"That is an interesting statement. I would like you to explore those feelings."

"Well, there are things men just don't talk about and being afraid of anything is a big one. I would never admit to anyone that I was afraid, but Brock did it without any hesitation."

"That is called vulnerability. We are all vulnerable and you come from a generation of fathers with the belief that men don't cry. How much of their teaching gets passed onto the next generation varies. Did you hear statements like those from your father when you were growing up?"

"I think that was one of Dad's favourite statements. He saw any show of emotion as a weakness and I wasn't allowed to show any sign of weakness or he made fun of me. I could never go to him when I was most afraid and that is when I really needed someone to talk to. He saw boys crying as a weakness and for years, I used to cry myself to sleep at night so no one could see me. No one knew. You're the first person I have ever told."

"You never told your mother?"

"No, I knew she would tell Dad and I didn't want him to make fun of me."

"You haven't mentioned this to Martha?"

"No, I was too ashamed to mention anything like that to her."

"Do you think she would think less of you?"

"I never really thought about it. I guess it was a way of life by then and I never even considered it."

"You said you were ashamed. Can you tell me more about your shame?"

"I've never talked about it and I've hidden it for so long, I don't know."

"I think it's important to talk about this shame. Can you trust me?"

"You haven't laughed at me yet, so I guess so. Its just hard for me."

"Do you know why it is hard for you?"

"I have buried it so I wouldn't hurt. I try not to think about it. There were times when my memories of it hurt so bad, I wished there was someone to talk to but there never was. Sometimes I feel so alone." Grant stopped and sat in quiet isolation. The true meaning of his last words hit him with a force he hadn't felt before. He started to cry. It was a quiet cry where he tried to hold back but his tears betrayed him. He wiped them away with the back of his hands, but that failed to manage the flow.

Anne moved the box of tissues closer thinking he had forgotten them. Grant ignored them. She suspected he was in that place where his mind was dealing with the pain and the eyes just wouldn't focus.

Grant discerned the movement and realized where he was. His pain came rushing back. He looked away from Anne.

"What would it mean if you did talk about it?"

Grant thought about what it did mean to him and his head was swimming in a pool of fear. "That is a hard question. I have hidden it for so long; talking about it was not ever an option. Fear always closed the door to even consider it." Grant sat and pondered his statements and Anne could see he was about to add to his answer, so she gave him the time he needed. "I guess that if I started to talk about it, it would be real. If it is real, there will be more questions and I don't know if I have the answers. Maybe I'm afraid of the answers. Everything about this tells me if I don't talk about it, I will be able to manage living my life. If I did tell, would anyone even believe me?" As he spoke, his shoulders sagged and he avoided looking at Anne.

"These feelings are very normal. Fear can have a great power over our lives. Did you ever consider talking to a priest or someone in your church?"

Grant jolted upright and snapped his head back to look directly at Anne, tears and all. His face went rigid and flushed a dark crimson. While holding her look, he unfolded himself from his chair and began pacing back and forth in the small available space. After a few rotations, he sought out a corner and stood facing away from Anne.

She watched in analytical wonder and knew he needed time.

An abrupt wail signified his break into uncontrolled spasmodic sobbing.

Anne watched Grant's shoulders shake and began to confirm her guess as to what had happened to cause this reaction.

He quieted. His anguish was palpable. He fought to turn but he couldn't face her. He whispered. "A priest was the cause of my shame." His shoulders showed defeat.

Anne walked over careful not to invade his space. She spoke in a calming voice, "Grant, can you trust me to be the first person to hear your story?" She let him have time to process her words. The long seconds turned into minutes. She waited.

Grant felt Anne's presence. Her soft voice, so full of compassion put him at ease. His mind was replaying her words. Trust, that is what he needed. Could he trust her? He was torn. She had never broken his trust and he shared things with her he hadn't shared with many people. Yes, he could trust her, but could he trust himself? "I don't know if I can talk about what happened."

"Take your time and only go as far as you're comfortable. You set the pace. As we are exploring, you tell me if you need to stop."

He heard what she said and kept repeating inside his head, '*I can trust her, I can trust her, I can trust her.........*' until he turned and looked her in the eyes. His face, wracked with dismay, was betrayed by his voice which was laced with hope. "I will try. I just don't know how far I can go."

The contract was made. Anne was hopeful this session would open doors to his healing. Grant took his seat while Anne gave him a challenge, "Think about where you want to start. The important journey we are about to take is not the easiest. We can work through the rest of this session and the next session is available so we could have time if we needed it. You are still in control, I just wanted to create an environment where you wouldn't be cut off because time was running out." She took her seat, "Where do you want to start?"

"Thank you. I guess it would help me if I give you some background. Is that okay?" Grand looked for her approval.

Anne saw the change that had overtaken him, and she wanted to keep him talking. "That is a great place to start." She settled back with open body language to make him comfortable.

"When I was three, our church received a young parish priest, Father Michael O'Hara. We called him Father Mike and Mom and Dad took him under their wings to welcome him into the neighbourhood. They invited him over to the house all the time and I grew up knowing him like family." He paused and questioned himself if he could do this. He wasn't sure.

Anne felt his anxiety and thought she would soften the mood, "So you saw Father Mike as a member of your family. Did your parents encourage you to view him this way?"

"No, he was just always there so he naturally became like a member of our family to me. We got to know him very well. He also got to know us. He was a great guy, was good looking, and very likeable. I remember all the single girls in the church nicknamed him '*Father What-a-Waste*'." Grant smiled at the last statement.

Anne chuckled. "Yes, we used to use that for good-looking priests too." She saw Grant relax and encouraged him to continue. "Can you tell me more about him?"

"He wasn't like any other priest we ever had, he was fun to be around. People would often tell each other that we should count our blessings to have gotten a priest like him. He seemed to be the engaging, energetic power that our church was missing. He knew how to connect with people and was the catalyst for getting people involved. Community leaders were encouraged to run the programs he developed around what people said they wanted. He had a '*why not*' attitude when people asked for something to be run in the church; he was always willing to try something. His role was to oversee but he would also lead programs when no one would come forward. The church grew under his leadership so there was something for everyone. Everyone loved him; Mom, Dad, neighbours, other church members all paid him accolades on what a great guy he was. I attended several programs over the years, and I enjoyed the camaraderie we experienced because of them. He seemed to bring the community together."

Grant seemed calm so she reviewed what he had said. "So, Father Mike encouraged participation in the community?"

Grant answered without needing to think, "He did, and we were all encouraged to join in. He was real. He always seemed interested in what I was doing and spent quality time with me. He was more of a father than Dad was." Grant paused and looked away as if thinking back.

119

Anne saw this and summarized, "It sounds like you had a strong relationship with him."

"I did, until he ruined it." It was out of his mouth before he realized it. He froze.

Anne saw his reaction and knew this was a crucial moment. He could freeze up or open up. She needed him to start talking again and cautiously asked, "Are you ready to talk about that?"

"No, I don't think I can." He answered abruptly.

Anne was a little surprised at his tone but knew this was not going to be easy. "Grant, I believe whatever happened between you and Father Mike needs to be explored. We can do it when you are ready."

He sputtered, "I'm not ready, I just can't. Not today."

"Can we explore it next session?"

"I will try to be ready to do that, but I can't make any promises."

"You are in control, Grant. We will go at whatever pace you need to."

"Thank you for being so understanding. I will see you next week." He got up to leave.

Anne walked him out, said goodbye, and watched him walk down the hall hoping he would turn around. After the door closed, she leaned her back against it and thought about his pain.

Chapter 30

Brock took the Saturday off from 'the Manor' as it was a light day. The guests were staying another day and the guys could manage the touch-up very well. Mammie's garden, now his, was in good shape having benefitted from his mourning for Mammie. He found comfort in the gardens when he was feeling down, and he spent many hours thinking of her while he cleaned up from the winter and enjoyed watching the green growth emerge from their winter's rest. The bulbs he had planted for her last fall were filling the garden with hundreds of buds. The daffodils in the sunnier parts of the garden were almost done blooming, and the tulip buds were starting to push toward the sky.

He and Matthew planned to spend the day together. They created a small list of things they wanted to get done. They kept the list manageable so they would have some time to be together without anything else taking up their time. To make sure they got quality time together, they put it at the top of their list. They had learned this from Andrew. He was not known as 'Mr. List' for nothing.

They finished a few small jobs and were doing a general tidying up of the house. They were storing things away in the same closet with the Christmas decorations. Matthew became excited, "Brock, you have all the ornaments we used to decorate Mammie's tree! Are you going to use them as your own?"

"It seems funny to say but they are mine. Mammie gave me everything. I never even gave it a thought until you asked but yes, I will use them. When I think back to that night when we decorated her tree and the joy she was having as she unwrapped each ornament and told its story, I will treasure those memories and the ornaments the rest of my life."

"Can we plan a special Christmas for us this year? It will be our first."

Brock smiled at his excitement, "It's a little early but I think that is a great idea."

"It is almost seven months away; it will be here before we know it!" His words made him even more excited.

"Okay, over that time we will need to think of the special things we want to include as we define our Christmas tradition."

Matthew hugged Brock, "Thank you! One thing I don't want is a lot of gifts; I think it is gross how people buy so much stuff. That is not what Christmas is about for me. How do you feel?"

Brock smiled, "I'm in complete agreement. Let's keep it small and concentrate on those things that are important. We can define our Christmas to fit us."

Matthew nodded, "The other day, I was talking with a couple from church and they use a simple formula that I thought was really unique. I would like us to consider using it. Are you game?"

Brock looked puzzled, "I guess it depends what this formula is."

"It's really simple. We each get the other four gifts; one in each of the following categories: something you want, something you need, something to wear, and something to read."

Brock's face lit with a big smile. "That's brilliant! I love the idea."

Matthew added, "We will both be in university, and we won't have much money. Can I add that all four gifts cannot cost more than $50 in total?"

Brock forgot that Matthew didn't know about his wealth, it had completely slipped his mind. He continued, "A fifty-dollar limit will be an interesting challenge to work with! I would also like to add that gifts don't have to be new. If we find something good that is second-hand, I would love that we recycle good used things!"

"Me too!" Matthew was overcome with excitement. One would think he was a child, and it was Christmas Eve.

Brock enjoyed his enthusiasm and ruffled his hair. "Matthew, I really love who you are!"

*****

It was unseasonably warm for the end of May, but no one was complaining after the cold winter. The city was alive with activities and people were out everywhere. They got their work done by lunch and had the rest of the day to enjoy each other's company.

"How about we walk over to the City Market and get an ice cream?" suggested Matthew.

"That would be nice but how about taking a drive on this beautiful day?" Brock countered.

"Will we be driving by a place to get ice cream? The City Market is wonderful, but I was really more interested in getting ice cream. So, if we can do that while we are out driving, I'm game!"

"Well, St. Martins has a great ice cream bar, and we can stop there. How about we drive out to the Fundy Trail? We could pack a picnic lunch and make a fun day of it."

"Great idea Brock, I love picnics! Let's put some food together and get going!" Matthew was excited.

They had gotten groceries the night before, so the snacks were plentiful and in 10 minutes they had their picnic lunch packed in Mammie's antique picnic basket and put it in the car. "Mammie would be so pleased we are using her basket. When I was about ten, she packed it with a proper lunch, and we sat in the backyard on a blanket and had a picnic. The same blanket I just put in the car. She was so full of fun!" Brock ended as his face crumbled and tears flowed down his cheeks. "I really miss her!"

Matthew went over to him and drew him into a hug, "She was so special to you. I'm a little jealous of your relationship with her. I don't have anyone like that in my life."

"What about me?"

You don't count as someone like Mammie. Our relationship is so very wonderfully different. We have sex!" Matthew smiled and winked.

Brock acted out mock shock, "Matthew!"

"Well, its true isn't it? You never had sex with Mammie." Matthew chuckled.

"That's enough of your warped mind. Get in the car and we can take off."

*****

On the drive, the car picked up Brock's music on his phone. Within seconds Abba's 'Dancing Queen' blew out of the speakers. Brock started singing along and Matthew joined in at the top of his lungs.

Brock looked over at Matthew with surprise. He ignored Brock except for a wink, kept singing and added hand movements. The adventure had begun.

Several tunes saw them out of town and well on their way to St. Martins when Matthew turned the music off after the song, that was playing, ended. "This is so gay, and I'm loving it! A year ago, would you believe you would be driving in your own car with your own boyfriend?"

"No, a year ago I got a job at a B&B owned by two gay men and I freaked out that people would tease me. We've come a long way!" Brock puckered and kissed the air for Matthew.

"You've had a lot of good but there were bad things too. I still find it surreal that your parents kicked you out. I see your mom has changed in her thinking and your dad is coming around, but he is still struggling. Can you imagine holding beliefs that are so wacked that strongly that you couldn't let go?"

Brock thought about it. "I guess we all have beliefs that could be wacked. I can't think of any that I have but I just may not be aware. If I did, I would hope that I was open enough to educate myself and become more evolved."

"Something has a hold on your dad and we just aren't aware of what that could be. Heck, he might not even be aware. I hope he figures it out soon." Matthew stopped and was in thought for a few minutes before saying, "The fact that your dad went to the Pflag meeting though is a great first step."

"Yes, I'm not comfortable around him yet. Being in the same room with him at the Pflag meeting was something I never expected after they kicked me out. A lot has happened since my birthday."

"Your dad brings an edge into the room that is hard to be comfortable around. You never know what he is thinking."

They talked throughout their walk on the Fundy Trail about many subjects. Every so often something would come up that they hadn't discussed before. They were learning more new things about each other.

They found a deserted beach covered with thousands of round rocks. They learned they both liked rocks that were different, and the uniqueness of this space told them it was the perfect place to eat their lunch. The sun was beating down on them and they removed their shirts to start a tan. Matthew's workouts, that were supervised by Brock, were showing results. Where once there was no definition, muscles were evident, and he had the start of a six pack. You couldn't say he was ripped but he was on his way! Brock complimented him, "Look at you! Soon you'll have all the great-looking guys after you!"

"Thank you Brock, but I have the only great-looking guy I want in my life."

They got back to the car by four o'clock and drove down into the village for ice cream. "Here we are, your ice cream awaits!" Brock said as he pulled into the shop and killed the ignition.

"What flavour are you having? What is your favourite ice cream?" Matthew asked.

Brock had his answer as soon as the question was asked, "I love Mint Chocolate Chunk. If they have it, that makes my choice easy. What about you?"

"I like Mint Chocolate Chunk too, but my all-time favourite is Heavenly Hash. I hope they have it!"

They both were in luck and soon were eating their cones on the drive home.

Brock's phone sounded with Mackenzie's ringtone and the Bluetooth answered it. " Hello Sis!"

"Where are you right now?" There was something in her voice.

"We are out by Costco, what's up?"

"Dad has been rushed to hospital by ambulance and Mom went with him. They think t might be his heart. I'm taking their car and heading over. We would like you to come."

"I'm heading there right now. We will meet you in the '*Outdoor*'." He looked over at Matthew, but he didn't need to ask.

Without hesitation, Matthew responded, "I'm going with you."

Chapter 31

As Brock and Matthew walked into the hospital, Matthew queried, "Why do we Saint Johners refer to the Emergency Room as the '*Outdoor*'?"

Brock responded as the doors closed behind him, "I don't know but it has always been the '*Outdoor*' in our family. We'll have to check this out sometime." They walked into the waiting area and saw Mackenzie, "There she is!"

Mackenzie ran over and hugged Brock and Matthew. "I'm so glad you're here. Dad had not been feeling well since last night. He even missed his therapy session this morning. He was having a pain in his chest and told Mom there was a pressure as if something was sitting on his chest. He also had a sore left shoulder with pain going down his arm. Mom Googled heart attack symptoms and, when she read through them, she said she wasn't fooling around, so she called the ambulance. She then called me at my friend's place and asked me to meet them here...."

She hadn't finished her sentence before Brock jumped in, "Have you heard anything about his condition?"

"Mom is in with him and they are doing tests. Once they are completed and if they will allow it, we could go in then."

Matthew interjected, "This is a family time, and I don't want to be in the way. I would like to stay with you, but you want to be just the two of you, no biggie, I can go home."

Brock looked at Mackenzie who spoke up, "Putting up with my brother qualifies you as family to me. I would love to have you stay if you want."

While they waited, Mackenzie told them about hanging out with Lisa and they told her about their hike and picnic at the Fundy Trail. Matthew ended the summary by explaining their special Christmas idea and the more he talked the more excited he became.

"I really like those four gift categories. I think society has gone gift crazy and they have made Christmas very materialistic. I think we should all …." Mackenzie stopped short when her mother called their names from the side doors. She was holding the doors so they didn't lock. The security guard saw what was going on and went over. Martha hugged each of the kids, even Matthew, "Hi Matthew, I'm glad you are here with Brock."

She spelled it out for the guard, "My husband is in room 7 and my kids are coming with me." He ushered them into the Emergency room and left them outside room 7.
Martha wanted to update the kids before they went in, "The tests were inconclusive, so they have done more tests. They are treating it as a heart attack, just in case, until they know differently. They want to get the results from those tests before they give us a diagnosis. It could be many hours or tomorrow. He has had medication so he is groggy, and he may not wake up while we are in there. Are you ready?" They all nodded, and Martha led the way, "Let's go see him."

It was a shock for the kids to see their father in the hospital bed. He was so pale, and tubes and wires were seemingly coming out of everywhere. He heard someone come in and opened his eyes just enough to see who was there. In a weak voice, "Hi."

Mackenzie went first, "Hi Dad, we came over to make sure you were behaving yourself." She looked to Brock.

He was reluctant as to what he needed to say but came up with, "Matthew and I were out to the Fundy Trail today and were just coming back to town when we heard. Are you in any pain?"

Grant's eyes closed but fluttered open again and spoke in that low voice, "No,…….. good drugs." His eyes closed again but stayed closed this time.

All four stood in silence watching him. After a few minutes, Martha spoke, "That is the extent of his communication since they administered the drugs. I don't know what it is, but he cannot stay awake for more than a few minutes each hour. When he does wake, he doesn't say much before dropping off again. I don't think you need to stay here for long. It would be good for you to go home and get your sleep." She looked to Mackenzie, "Would you put a change of clothes for me in a bag and bring them over, I will spend the night here."

Mackenzie nodded, "I will do that. Is there anything else you might need?"

"I would like my iPad. That will keep me occupied during his sleep time. I've heard some people have a cot brought in, but I'm not sure they will do that in the 'Outdoor.' I might just sit up in that chair; I'll see."

Brock thought for a few seconds and offered, "When I would sit with Mammie, I found the chair very versatile. When I wanted to sleep, I sat near the bed and laid my head on a pillow on the side of the bed next to her. It wasn't that bad."

Martha nodded, "I'll try that. I just think the cot might get in the way if they needed to check on Dad."

"It is getting late, so I'll run and get your stuff. Maybe I will leave the car here for you in case you want to go home. It is parked at the spot right near the stairs. Brock can take me and bring me back – right Bro?" Mackenzie looked to her brother.

Brock jumped right in, "Sure, we can go right away. Mom, have you eaten anything?"

"I did have lunch but that is all. I haven't had an appetite since this happened."

"We have some food left over from our picnic lunch that would be a whole lot better than anything you will get in this hospital. I will go get it and bring it in before we go."

"There is no need to bring any food in right now but when you come back, I would probably be ready to eat something then."

Brock took the lead, "Okay, let's go. Love you Mom!" Brock and Mackenzie said together while Matthew said, "Bye Mrs. Matheson."

*****

Martha awoke to find Grant watching her. "Hi Sweetheart, how are you feeling?"

Grant responded, "I'm feeling okay. Do they know what is wrong with me yet?"

"No, they haven't come with the results of those additional tests. I hope we get them today."

"How are you feeling, Martha. You must be exhausted?"

"Actually, I'm feeling better than I thought I would. I wasn't expecting to get much rest, but I managed quite well sleeping most of the night."

"I was watching you sleep when I was overwhelmed with the love I have for you. I don't know if you will ever know how much I love you."

"Oh, Grant, I love you too and I want you to get better."

"I was laying here thinking about Dad. He had a stroke in May the year I was in grade twelve. It is May and Brock is in grade twelve. Is the universe telling me something? I couldn't get it out of my mind and realized that he died three years later. That got me to wonder how long I have left."

"I hope we have many years left. When the doctor tells us, we can plan to live the best life we can."

The door opened and a doctor entered. "Grant Matheson, I am Doctor Susan Turrell. I reviewed the results of your tests with a team of doctors trying to make sense of what got you in here. I am happy to tell you we can rule out stroke and heart attack. When you arrived, you were complaining of chest pains and told us that your father had died of a heart attack.

We ran preliminary tests, and they showed no heart issues, but we wanted to rule heart attack out completely, so we did the second set to make sure. When your wife talked to us, she told of the great stress you and your family has been under and we believe the chest pain you were experiencing was the result of anxiety and stress."

He looked at her and then at Martha, "I have been under more stress in the last four months than I have had the rest of my life." He hadn't told Martha about having to leave last week's therapy session because of the panic he was feeling. Then, as yesterday's therapy session approached, he found himself panicking more and more frequently. He was relieved when Martha cancelled because he wasn't feeling well.

The doctor went on to describe the symptoms that anxiety and stress can cause, and Grant saw himself in all that she said. He listened as the doctor spoke and when she said that if a patient cannot get the stress or anxiety under control, it could lead to a number of serious health conditions.

She gave him a list of things he could do to manage the stress and anxiety. See a therapist was one that stood out for Grant and he silently made a commitment to see Anne and finish what he started.

The doctor finished and said she would go do the paperwork to send him home recommending he take a few days off and try some of the relaxation techniques spelled out in the documents she gave him.

As she left the room, Mackenzie and Brock entered and they each gave both parents hugs. When Brock went to his father's bedside, he hesitated but Grant reached out and wrapped him in his muscled arms. It took a few seconds, but Brock relaxed into the hug.

Mackenzie was first to remark, "Dad, you look a lot better than you did last night. Did you get your results?"

Grant nodded and explained what the doctor had said about his chest pains. He told them he was taking the next few days off and would try to de-stress. "I was wondering if we could start having family suppers every Sunday. I really miss having us all together and I think it is time to start putting things to right. Yes, Brock I want you to be part of the family again. Will you come?"

Brock was surprised by this turn of events and sputtered, "Yes I want to be there if you want me there. I've wanted this since my birthday! I miss my family."

"I do. I have a lot to learn and I'm finally going to educate myself. He looked over to Mackenzie and said, "Mackenzie has frequently reminded me, on many different occasions, that I need to change my ways. I ask that you please be patient while I explore a new me."

Martha couldn't believe what Grant had said but overcame her surprise to say, "I want Dad to rest up today so, a week from today, I expect to see everyone at home for supper.

Come early, say four o'clock, and we can spend time together before supper."
Each one nodded in agreement and there were smiles all round.

Chapter 32

Grant walked into Anne's office and found her looking through her appointment book at the receptionist's desk. "Hi Anne, I'm sorry I had to cancel last week's session. I was having chest pains and when they got worse throughout the day, I ended up in the '*Outdoor*.' They thought I was having a heart attack but after a bunch of tests they determined it was stress."

"How are you feeling now?"

"I am feeling well. The hospital stay did me a lot of good."

"Oh? Let's go sit. I can't wait to hear what good came out of it."

They moved into the therapy room and each took their chairs. Anne asked, "So the hospital did you a lot of good. Tell me more."

"While I lay in the bed waiting for the diagnosis, I thought about life. Being told that they were checking my heart sent me into a spin. Dad had a stroke in May when I was in grade twelve and I had to leave school to take over his business. He only lived a few more years before dying of a heart attack. I got to thinking it is May and Brock is in grade twelve and I was in hospital for what could have been a heart attack, so it made me really look at my life. I wasn't pleased with what I saw. I have been pig-headed. I want to make amends for the damage I have done to my family and I know you are the one to help me do this. No matter how hard this is for me, I give you permission to do whatever you need to do to get through this thick head of mine. One thing I need to tell you is that Father Mike hurt me badly, and I have been hiding it for the past thirty years. I need your help to deal with the hurt; it is killing me."

Anne heard his words like a breath of fresh air. He was ready! "Sometimes something happens to help people move forward with their work. I guess your almost heart attack was yours."

"The way I see it is that I have been given a second chance. I have watched the news over the years and the Catholic Church has been dealing with abuse by priests, but I have difficulty calling our relationship abusive. I want to help you understand who I thought Father Mike was so you will see what I'm talking about."

Anne was pleased to get over that hump. "Okay, tell me who Father Mike was."

He started off slowly, "Like I said last time, he came into our lives early on and became a friend of the family. I always looked forward to him coming over to our house." He paused, again reflecting on what he had said. "Sometimes he minded me when Mom and Dad went out for the evening and those times were special. He read me stories, we played a variety of games, and he seemed to genuinely care about me. I liked him a lot, you could even say I loved him like a father, I mean a dad. He paid attention, he remembered what I was doing and would ask me about things, something my father never did." Grant stopped, looked at Anne with a blank look and shook his head. His face crumbled and tears flowed down his cheeks. He didn't attempt to wipe them away.

Anne wondered what she could do next to keep him going. It was clear the pain he was feeling was the result of a trust being broken and she needed to explore that. "Tell me about your father, Grant."

Grant took a few minutes to consider his answer. "Dad was around the house, but he wasn't an active part of my life. If he loved me, I never knew. I don't think he knew much about me. He was a cold man who didn't show me any affection. There were a lot of years when I didn't like him, I could even say I hated him because punishment was the only attention I received. There was never any encouragement or positive feedback. Father Mike, on the other hand, did everything Dad didn't and it felt good to have someone interested in me. He was a positive role model and I looked up to him. I guess I put him on a pedestal. I couldn't wait until I could see him again." Grant paused again, remembering how good life with Father Mike was.

Anne noted that in the response about his father, Grant brought Father Mike into it in a positive way. This confused her, was Father Mike the abuser or not? She needed more information to sort things out. She needed to keep him talking. "Father Mike seemed to replace your father, is that what you are trying to say?"

Grant looked perplexed. He started to say something and stopped three separate times and pushed himself to say, "He was everything my father wasn't, and he provided me with the emotional role model I now know I didn't have. My father was always too busy to spend time with me, but Father Mike went out of his way to make time for me. I ate up the one-on-one attention Father Mike would give me. Dad must have believed that positive feedback would make me soft because he only told me what I was doing wrong or berated the way I did something. Father Mike was the opposite, he lavished me with positive feedback. Dad was not affectionate; there were never any hugs. He would never think of putting a hand on my shoulder to tell me I did something well; he was so old school. Father Mike always met Mom and me with hugs when he visited. He brought a new kind of freedom; one of expressive emotion that I had never seen from any man in my life. He seemed too good to be true. Personally, the most important thing was that he was there for me." Grant stopped abruptly as if something he remembered was too painful to say out loud. A long silence ensued.

Anne let the silence sit in the room hoping Grant would continue. When he didn't, she interjected. "I am getting that you cherished that relationship. Would you say you did?"

Grant realized she had asked a question. "I'm sorry. I was off in another world and didn't hear what you said."

Anne repeated her question.

"I think everyone cherished their relationship with him. I know I idolized that man. My parents encouraged me to become an altar boy and were proud of having a son in the church. Not that they ever told me, but I overheard them talking about it to others when they didn't know I was listening. It was all so new and wonderful. Then we ruined it." Grant stopped and sat thinking.

Anne let the silence happen but when it went on too long, she wanted to explore, "You said we ruined it. Who are the we?"

"Father Mike and I."

"What did you ruin and how did you ruin it?"

"We ruined it all. All the wonderful feelings I had were gone in one afternoon or at least they were brought into question by my mind."

"Can you tell me what happened that afternoon?"

"I don't know if I can; I may need your guidance. I will try my best; I'm committed to getting this talked about."

"Please try. Start slowly and stop anytime you need to."

"Okay. Altar serving was a bonus for me because I got to spend time with Father Mike. I would do anything to be around him more. After serving at the church the other altar boys would change out of their robes and leave but I would stay back. Father Mike would have me go to the First Aid room at the back of the church hall while he closed up the church. It was a small room with a cot, two chairs, and some first-aid supplies. When he arrived, he would sit in one of the chairs and I sat across from him on the cot. We spent our time talking and they were special talks; we explored many topics and I was able to ask him anything knowing he wouldn't ridicule me. Father Mike never made me feel dumb. We would laugh and talk about everything while we ate the treats he always brought. That was our time together and I loved the attention. I felt so special." He paused, took a drink of water and sat thinking.

Anne put what she heard into her own words as a kick start. "Time with Father Mike was very special to you and you took every chance you could get to be with him. Is that a fair statement?"

"It is very true. I didn't have much of a relationship with Dad and I enjoyed being with Father Mike. Then came the day that changed things in a way I never fully understood until much later." He paused again but looked off into nowhere.

"Take your time. I'm here when you are ready."

Grant straightened his posture as if steeling himself to fend off an unknown foe. He started. "That day started off like any of the many times we had together but this day, he began a conversation about puberty. At eleven, I knew little about sex and told him I didn't know what he was talking about. He told me about how boys mature and explained the changes that take place. I felt proud to tell him that I experienced those changes, body hair and erections. He told me about masturbation and how it was a natural part of growing up. He asked if I masturbated. I lied and said I hadn't because I knew, from friends, that it was a sin. I didn't want to admit that sin to a priest who heard my confessions. When I blushed, he knew and told me it was alright to talk about it. He crossed the room and sat next to me on the cot. He sat so close I could feel his body heat. He put his arm over my shoulder and spoke to me in a comforting way, softly whispering close to my ear. I opened up and told him that I did masturbate, and he prompted me to tell him about my feelings and what I thought about while I masturbated. With him being so close, his body heat, and his soft voice tickling my ear, my body responded, and I got an erection. I was embarrassed that he might notice. And notice he did. He reminded me that an erection was natural part of growing to be a man. He shared that he would get them sometimes during a mass, but they were his secret because he was able to hide them under his gowns. I was surprised and we giggled. He then told me he had one too and I looked at his crotch to see a bulge.

I guess I stared too long because he took my hand and placed it on his pants saying, '*It looks like you are interested, go ahead and feel it.*' I was in shock and mesmerized at the same time. He kept whispering that it was okay to touch it. All I remember thinking was that this was Father Mike so it must be okay. No one had ever talked to me about sex before, so I trusted that if he said it was okay, it was." Grant stopped and sat there in numbness.

Anne knew they were close and needed to keep him going so she prompted, "Are you okay to continue?"

"All I knew was that he told me it was okay, so I went along. He said it was okay."

"You trusted him."

"Yes, I trusted him more than anyone in my life. I had never seen an erection other than my own and to touch his excited me. I'm embarrassed to say that but that is how it felt. Does that make me gay?" He made a furrowed-brow frown and looked at her with pleading eyes.

"Are you attracted to men?"

"No, I'm attracted to women."

"Then you aren't gay. Sexual orientation is all about who you are sexually attracted to and you are attracted to the opposite sex, so you are heterosexual."

"But I touched his erection and I remember the excitement. I wasn't repulsed. How do you explain that?"

"The body responds to stimulation and it doesn't matter what the gender of the person is, the penis responds. Did you ever get a spontaneous erection as a child?"

Grant blushed, "You do ask personal questions but yes, all the time; sometimes putting me in awkward situations."

"This is nothing to be embarrassed about, it is all perfectly normal. Those erections are examples of the stimulation that happens and no matter how hard you try to not have the erection, it happens anyway. Does this help?"

"Yes, I think it helps a lot."

Anne could see the toll that the session was taking on Grant; he looked utterly exhausted. She wondered if he would be able to finish. "You're beat, would you like to stop, or do you want to continue?"

"I am beat, but I need to do this." He sat there wondering if he had the energy to go further but he remembered laying in the hospital bed and was determined to finish. "I remember feeling his erection and realized it was so much bigger than my own. I was curious but afraid at the same time. It made me harder. He whispered soothing words in my ear. It tickled and tingled and excited me even more. I was feeling all of the excitement as he undid my zipper. I didn't try to stop him. He took my erection out with his big, warm, soft, hand and rubbed it ever so lightly. Feelings coursed through my body and I was ready to explode. He must have sensed it because he bent down and took it into his mouth and the moist suction drove me over the edge; the need was so strong. If I felt that it was wrong, I wasn't aware, I was overcome with feelings I had never felt before. When he sat up, he opened his fly and placed my hand around his erection. He told me to treat his erection as if it was mine and guided me to masturbate him. The hardness and warmth felt good in my hand and he kept saying that he liked it. He told me to put it in my mouth. I resisted until he gently directed my head down onto it. He guided me in what he wanted me to do. He was loud when he climaxed. Afterward, I sat gathering my thoughts; they were coming from all directions. He held me in a tight hug while he told me how special I was and how much this time together meant to him. We adjusted our clothing and talked more. He told me that this would be our secret and I was not to tell anyone. He said if people knew, they wouldn't let us have special times together. I was conflicted deep down but kept telling myself it must be okay because Father Mike said it was."

"What did you do after leaving him?"

"I went home for supper. All the way home I replayed what had happened and I tried to sort out how I felt."

"How did you feel?"

"I guess the best description is that I was bewildered, no one had ever talked about this to me. I had experienced so many new feelings; some that felt so good and some that caused me much confusion. The whole situation had me questioning so many things that would take months and years to put some answers around. I guess I was too green to understand the depth of what had happened. What kept me going was that Father Mike and I shared something only the two of us knew about and it was our special secret. He had chosen me."

"Did you mention what you did to your parents or anyone else?"

"No, I did what Father Mike told me to do. I kept it a secret."

"How are you feeling right now?"

"My head is aching, and I am exhausted, but I feel oddly lighter."

"Can you explain the 'oddly lighter' part to me?"

"I have been carrying the burden of what happened for over thirty years dreading the thought of talking about it to anyone. I feel I was used by Father Mike; I don't know if it would be called abuse. You allowed me the time I needed, and you didn't judge me. I think that was my biggest fear. Talking about it with honesty and not having to colour my story took a load off my back. Thank you for helping me through this."

"You are welcome, but I believe we have only just begun. It is abuse Grant, you were a child, and he was an adult. It wasn't your fault, it was his. We will be exploring more in the next session. Are you willing to go the next step?"

"As I told you the story, I reflected on parts of it. I think this is behind my negative beliefs about gays. Yes, I'm willing to go the next step with you. I need to for Brock's sake."

"I am glad you are doing this. How is your family doing?"

"After my revelation in the hospital, we discussed having family Sunday dinners with Brock and Mackenzie and our first one is tomorrow."

"That is a big move. Who came up with that idea?"

"I did. It dawned on me that I was missing out on my son's life because of attitudes that I'm now seeing are old and outdated. A big part of me is the way my father behaved and that doesn't make me feel very good. I thought a good first step would be to start getting together around the supper table and testing out my new evolving views."

Anne was amazed with what she was hearing, "Grant, Martha must be ecstatic! You have come a long way since we first met. I am so pleased."

"She is very pleased; I think she does not believe it is happening. I've realized that with your help and a near-death experience anything can happen!"

"Once there is a desire to change, then anything can happen. Have a great week and see you next Saturday."

Chapter 33

Brock held the phone in front of him and counted the rings as he waited for his mother to answer.

"Hi Brock, you haven't changed your mind, have you?"

"No, Mom, I was calling to see if Dad had changed his mind. Are we really getting together as a family today?"

"Yes, we really are getting together. Dad is in a good mood and looking forward to having you here. I tell you, that health scare really changed him. You'll see."

"I hope so. I can't help but think that we are going to be sitting around the table as a family for the first time since I was kicked out. It is a little freaky for me. I'm a little hesitant to go over, but I will be there."

"The table is the same but the people who will be around it are more evolved now, so just come over!"

"Okay Mom see you soon. Love you!"

Brock ended the call and thought about all the changes in his life in just a matter of months. He looked around his home – just thinking his home was different – and Mammie was everywhere but nowhere, and he felt deep sadness again that she was gone. He had made no plans to update the decorating yet but knew he wanted to make the place his someday. The thing that held him back is the thought that he would be obliterating Mammie's memory even though, logically, he knew it wouldn't. He remembered her saying that she would live on in his heart and he had to admit that was true. He gave some thought to going over to his parents' home, but something was stopping him. He couldn't say for sure, but he just didn't trust that he could start being a member of the family just like that. He guessed he would just have to see for himself and got his jacket.

He walked over to the door like he did hundreds, if not thousands, of times in the past when he left Mammie's place to go home. Today he had an ache in the pit of his stomach. He stood at the door and wondered if he should knock or just open the door and walk in. He turned the knob.

"Hi Son, I am so glad you are here! Now the family is back under one roof." His mother walked over and hugged him.

His father came into the kitchen, "It is good to see you Brock. Would it be okay if I gave you a hug?"

"It is more than okay." Brock met his dad halfway and wrapped his arms around him in a big hug. Before he let go he said, "I love you Dad."

"I love you too Son and I am sorry that it took this long to get the family back together. I suspect we will have awkward moments but if we both work through them; we can regain our original comfort."

They could hear Mackenzie's footsteps on the stairs. When she reached the bottom she yelled, "Is that my brother? I'm coming for a hug." She ran into the kitchen right into Brock's arms and clung to him. "I am so glad our family is together again!"

They stood around the kitchen filling each other in on the latest news each had, and a familiar comfort settled over the family.

When Brock went to set the table with his dad, he froze as he entered the dining room. Looking at each thing in the room brought a memory of that night. He looked to the wall for the hole from his punch; it had been repaired so you would never know it had been there, but his mind saw it in all of its raw emotional detail.

Later, when they were seated and eating, Martha brought a wrapped gift to the table. "This is your birthday present from Dad and me. Will you open it?"

Brock looked at the gift that she had just placed in front of him like she did on his birthday. He had a flashback but forced his brain to disconnect from it. He opened the card and read the front; '*Happy 18th Birthday Son*' and thought how ironic that the birthday was anything but happy. He quickly read the inside verse but got stuck on the signature, '*All our love, Mom & Dad*'. His brain brought judgemental thoughts that '*all their love*' wasn't enough to conquer their hatred of him being gay. He tried not to wallow, but he relived the pain as his father's words played in the background. Out of his fog came a voice.

"Go ahead Brock, open your gift." Martha slid it closer.

He shut down the memory of his birthday; he had to or he wouldn't be able to rejoin the family. He forced some wisdom that Mammie had given him in, '*You can't go back.*' He shook free of the negative energy, reached for the gift and tore off the wrappings. It was a box, he opened it. Inside he saw a sweater, and a book that he had wanted so badly for Christmas but didn't get. Life had been so crazy since that he had forgotten about it altogether. When he lifted the book, he noticed a small box tucked in the corner of the box. He lifted the hinged lid to see a simple gold ring with geometric marking around the band. He looked to his parents. "Thank you." As he examined the ring, something about it was familiar. "Dad, isn't this your ring? You wore it anytime you dressed up; is there a story?"

His father responded, "Yes, it was my ring, now it is yours. Your great grandmother gave it to your great grandfather on his 18th birthday about a year before they got married. He started a Matheson family tradition when he passed it on to your grandfather, my father, when he turned 18. He gave it to me on my 18th birthday and now I pass it on to you. You would have gotten it on your birthday if I hadn't messed everything up. I am sorry for that, but I want you to wear it with Matheson pride. Great grandmother had it inscribed, and I believe the inscription still holds true today; especially for us. Have a look."

Brock looked inside, "Let our love light your path." He smiled. "I guess my Great Grandmother was a wise woman."

"That she was."

Chapter 34

When the Mathesons attended the May Pflag meeting Andrew noticed a difference in their energy. Brock had told him of changes he had noticed in his dad's behaviours and how the Sunday family supper went well.

Grant had gone to Andrew before the meeting and asked if he could take some time to share something with Brock and his family in front of everyone. He explained his idea so Andrew would know what he intended doing.

Andrew thought about his request and responded, "I like the idea, but others are involved. I will put your request to the members and see if they are okay with you doing this." Andrew got the meeting going and was pleased when Grant spoke more than his name like he did at the last meeting during the introductions.

"Tonight, we have a request that I want each of you to consider. Grant would like to share information with his son in front of this group. This is a unique request and a unique opportunity to witness firsthand interaction between a father and son where the son was kicked out of the house and family when he came out. Is this something you would agree to spend some time on tonight? I would like to hear from you."

The room was quiet as they pondered what this could be.

Breanne broke the silence, "Personally, I would like to hear what Brock's father has to say. We could all learn something no matter which way it goes."

There were nods all around.

Mary spoke next, "As a parent who struggled with the same news, I would like to hear from another parent in a similar situation."

Redge added, "I would like to hear this too because I would like to understand how a dad could kick his child out of his life. It should be interesting."

The room went quiet and Andrew summarized, "It looks like we have some people willing to listen and then I saw nods, so I'm asking for a show of hands. Who would agree to have Grant take the floor?"

All hands shot up and Andrew spoke to Grant, "The floor is yours."

Grant cleared his throat without really knowing what he was so compelled to say and spoke, "As I said in my introduction, this is my second meeting. I didn't say a lot at the first meeting but tonight I have something I need to say. I started coming to these meetings because my wife gave me a couple of ultimatums, one about attending Pflag meetings and the other about going to see a therapist, both of which I didn't want any part of, but the cost of not doing them was too high.

I started with my therapist and have had weekly sessions for the past two months; the most recent was a special one I set for earlier today because of tonight. I knew I had lots of things to say but I wasn't sure I would say anything, so I needed the session to help me put my thoughts together. Over the past month I have been exploring the things I heard at the last meeting, especially the information Brock shared. Tonight, I am ready to address my behaviour.

Just admitting that is a big step for me. Last meeting, I listened as Brock spoke very openly about his fear. That is something I couldn't do until the therapist helped me. She helped me uncover a belief I had that expressing any kind of fear was unmanly and I was protecting my manliness at all cost. The trouble is, that behaviour almost cost me my family."

He looked at Brock, "Son, you have given me information I didn't know and this time I listened. The fact that you knew you were gay when you were a child was a concept that was hard for me to believe but I do believe you. That blows my theory that people choose to be gay. When you said that you went into the closet because of the things I said, it made me feel sad that I caused you so much pain. When you spoke about ignorant people, I thought you were talking about other people. When I finally realized that you were also talking about me, I didn't want to believe it even though Mackenzie tried to tell me that many times. I guess I needed to listen."

He looked at Mackenzie, "You actually said I was ignorant, and I dismissed what you were saying because I thought you were just being disrespectful. I didn't think you actually meant it. I thought you were lashing out at me. You know me well enough that I sometimes need to be hit over the head before I pay attention. I never dreamed I would say this but thank you for being unrelenting in making me see the truth."

He moved his glance to Martha, "I talked these things out with my therapist, and she helped me see things differently. I now know I was very ignorant and I'm working to open my mind. I feel I have failed my family, but thankfully you are more forgiving than I have been and are giving me another chance."

He paused and looked at each of the attendees, almost as if he was checking to see if they understood. He could tell they were listening, so he continued. "My therapist has helped me see the person I have been. I have disowned my only son, kicked him out of his home, and told him he was dead to me. I won't be up for '*Father of the Year*'. She had asked me why I had done that, and I thought long and hard, but I couldn't give her an answer. She doesn't accept non-responses and I knew she wouldn't let me off so easily, but I had no reasonable explanation for what I did. She didn't give up and tried a couple of approaches."

He stopped and looked at Mackenzie saying, "She is a lot like you in her determination to get me to see myself; you'd make a good therapist!

She pushed me, and I struggled. There were many times I wanted to walk out like I do at home when things get tough, but I now know that doesn't help anything. She helped me see a side of me that I was not aware of, and once I saw it, it was one I didn't like. I realized that having to admit to others that I had a gay son would have said something negative about me as a man; my concern for my reputation had me lashing out and giving Brock an unreasonable ultimatum. When I think about that night, I cringe at my response to you being honest with us. I now know it was ignorant and foolish of me, but I was tied up into what people would think of me as a man. I never gave any thought to what they might think of me as a father. When I look at the roles of man versus father, I now know that the role of father is so much more important and what my family thinks of me is more important than what anyone else thinks!

All of these realizations were a breakthrough for me today. That is a first step to becoming the new me. Although I have much more work to do, I am ready for the new me to be front and centre in my life. It's funny, my therapist told me she expected I would have been a tough nut to crack from what Martha had told her, but I believe the breakthrough blossomed from the foundation of very clear feedback that Mackenzie and Martha laid out for me even though, at the time, I didn't like it at all."

He looked at his wife, son, and daughter. "I'm so blessed to have three very intelligent people I am proud to call my family. I love you and I apologize for all the pain I have put you through. I ask you something I didn't offer you and that is, will you be patient with me? I feel I have only scratched the surface and I have so much more to learn, but I feel I'm ready. I am sure there will be some rocky roads ahead, but I promise I will listen to you and learn from you as we grow into our new and improved family."

The room broke into applause as Brock, followed by Martha and Mackenzie, stood and one by one hugged Grant. When they released, all four had tears streaming down their faces.

Grant continued standing as if he had something more to say. When the clapping subsided, he expressed a new learning, "I just realized that I can say I just came out of a closet too!"

The room filled with light laughter and Andrew allowed people to ask questions before continuing with the meeting.

"Thank you, Grant, for this unique opportunity. I am so pleased for you and your family. Now, we have about an hour left so are there any issues we need to explore with that time?"

Chapter 35

Grant had just finished telling Anne about what he did in the previous night's Pflag meeting and thanked her again for the special session he had with her before going to the meeting. He was about to move on when Anne stopped him with a question, "You have come a long way since we first met. Do you see why Martha and Mackenzie were so hard on you?"

"I do now but I was so tied to my old beliefs, I thought they were crazy."

"Why were you so tied to your old beliefs?"

"Because that is what I knew."

"Okay, why did you stick to those beliefs when so much information was coming out around same-sex marriage? You had to see the reasoning."

"It was cut and dried for me. If people tried to tell me anything different from what I believed, I really thought they were living in another reality, one that didn't connect with me."

"We can come back to this later. I know you don't like the word, but I want to explore the abuse. Are you okay with doing that?"

"I understood what you said about it being abuse so I can go along with the word. It is just that I am in a quandary about it. I made a commitment to deal with it so let's go."

"I want you to talk about the frequency of the abuse and how many weeks, months, or years that the sessions lasted."

"The sessions in the First Aid room were once or maybe twice a week. I was almost thirteen when they stopped." Grant fidgeted in his chair.

"Was it always at the church or did anything happen when he minded you?"

"Our special sessions started when I was eleven, mainly in the church but sometimes in our home."

"Did the activities you did change?"

145

"Not really. Sometimes we would masturbate ourselves or each other to climax and sometimes we only did oral sex. Many times, there was a mixture of both."

Up until then Grant was relaxed and looked her straight in the eyes as they talked. He was matter of fact with his answers and there wasn't any emotion. Anne wanted to get past this and into something that they could work on. She pressed. "How did it stop?" She saw something change in him. His hands started plying the material on the arms of the chair as he looked away to his left. She knew she had hit on something.

"One day, I had a dentist appointment, and I told Father Mike I wouldn't be there for Altar Service. The dentist got his work finished earlier than expected and I rushed to the church so we could have our session together. I ran as fast as I could and banged into the Bishop who had just entered the church hall. He asked me where I was running to and told him I had a meeting with Father Mike. He said he was looking for Father Mike too and asked me to take him there.

He followed me to the First Aid room while I explained that we had weekly sessions there. When I opened the door, a surprised Father Mike and Albert, another altar server, were in a state of undress and arousal. I gasped and sputtered not able to get any words out before the Bishop hugged me to his robes so I couldn't see what was happening. He told Albert to get dressed and leave. After he calmed me down, he told me to forget what I saw and to go home."

"What was going through your mind when you saw them?"

"It was a scene that I never expected to see but I have played it over and over in my mind since then. I was in turmoil. I didn't comprehend what was happening in the seconds after swinging the door open, but their images are burned into my brain. I asked myself many questions, but the answers were obvious, I just didn't want to believe them. The realization slowly sank in and I felt betrayed. I had been replaced. Then it hit; I wasn't special anymore and that pain crippled me. I stayed home sick for days and my parents didn't know what was wrong because I couldn't tell them. I was too ashamed. I cried myself to sleep every night for months, I missed Father Mike so much. I never saw him again. I started wondering how many other kids there were, and I went into a deep funk with the pain."

"How did your life change?"

"For a long while I was withdrawn and completely lost. I tried to carry on as if nothing had happened but the only male father figure that showed me any emotion was gone. I became quiet and reserved and Mom became worried about me. I would go to school but when I got home, I spent my time in the bedroom. I spent a couple of years believing nothing mattered anymore."

"You were probably mourning the end of that relationship. Did your parents take you to a doctor?"

"Yes, Mom did but the doctor told her I was a teen, and I would grow out of it. I didn't feel like I was taken seriously at all but then again, I never told anyone anything so how could they figure me out."

"Did the Bishop ever say anything to your parents?"

"If he did, I never knew. I do know he never mentioned it to me again. It was as if it hadn't happened. My world had been altered forever, but life went on as before only without Father Mike."

"When did things get better?"

"I couldn't keep going the way things were, the pain was too much so I decided to forget about it as best I could. I filled my time with school, football, and I started dating. Being on the football team I was able to have my pick of any of the girls that hung around the games and I conquered one after the other without going steady once. I used them for sex and left them. I got a reputation as a Casanova. If I had been female, I would have been called a slut. I was applauded for my prowess and girls wanted me."

"Looking back, do you think you were out to prove something?"

Grant furrowed his brow, "Like what?"

"That you weren't gay."

"If I was doing that, I wasn't aware. Sex with girls was a natural thing for me."

"Did what happened to you with Father Mike affect your relationships with men in general?"

"Not regular men but I grew to hate gay men. I was so disgusted with the thought of these men taking advantage of children I would lash out at them if one came near me."

"Do you believe gay men are child molesters?"

Grant looked at Anne as if she was losing her mind. 'Why wouldn't I? Father Mike was a child molester and he was gay."

"How do you know he was gay?"

Grant shook his head in disbelief and expelled a quick breath of frustration, "Anne, I am a little miffed with these questions. Haven't you been listening? He had sex with me. I am male and he is male so that makes him gay."

"Grant, all we know for sure is that he was a child molester, a paedophile. He may have also been gay, but we do not know that. You do not know what his sexual orientation was."

"I'm not getting it or you're not getting it, what am I missing?"

"Paedophilia is a sickness when adults or older teens molest children, usually younger than puberty but as old as thirteen so you fit in that upper category. It doesn't matter what their sexual orientation is. The distinction I need you to understand is being gay doesn't automatically make that person a child abuser." She watched him as he listened, and he started to frown. "What is going on in your mind Grant?"

"I think I remember something Martha said to me after returning home from a Pflag meeting. She told me that a father asked if all gays were paedophiles. She said something like '*it is generally accepted that approximately ten percent of the population is gay so approximately ten percent of teachers, police, doctors, politicians, etc. could be gay. Given that then approximately ten percent of paedophiles are gay.*' I thought she was being brainwashed at the Pflag meetings, but could that information be valid?"

"I have never heard it stated that way before, but I like how simple it addresses a difficult topic. Yes, I would say that description is valid."

"For years, I have equated gays to child molesters, and it isn't true."

"That's right Grant. How many of your other beliefs have proven not to be true?"

He hung his head and slowly shook it in realization of what he had done. "I don't know."

"What do you need to do now that you realize you could be wrong?"

"Mackenzie has been harping that I need to educate myself and although I hate to admit it, I think she is right. Can you help me with the right materials?"

"I can. Let's determine what areas you need help in, and I can identify appropriate resources."

Chapter 36

Brock went to 'the Manor' for work the morning after the Pflag meeting and found Andrew and Gregory in the kitchen.

Andrew brought up the meeting, "Hey Brock, what a powerful meeting for everyone who attended! I can't say I have ever seen such a dramatic change like the one your father has gone through and his honesty when he came out of his closet was poignant."

Brock nodded, "I never expected anything like what happened at the meeting. I guess his scare at the hospital and his therapy sessions had him thinking and he just opened up. I still find it hard to believe that the man who spoke last night was the same man who kicked me out just over four months ago. I give Mackenzie a lot of credit though, she has taken Dad to task several times since my birthday and has been relentless in speaking her mind. I believe little by little she has gotten him thinking and helped move him closer to what we saw last night. That and his health scare. Mom told me his hospital visit got him thinking and that is when we started to see the new Dad."

"It's simply an amazing turnaround. So, when do you tell your family you have a boyfriend?"

"I have to talk to Matthew about that. He didn't want anyone to know, so I'm not sure what he will think about coming out to my parents and not his."

"As always, you have lots to think about! As for today, all rooms have to be done up so you can go start with them."

"Is there anything special that I need to know?"

"No, it's just a regular day."

"Matthew might come over this afternoon. He wasn't sure if his parents wanted him to do anything, so we'll see."

Brock went to work on the rooms and had several things on the go at once. He occupied his mind with all that had happened the evening before and the growth that he has seen in his father. The first Sunday family supper was a little awkward at times with Brock not knowing what to expect but he had to say his father was trying. He asked about school and listened to his answer, he involved him in general conversation, and talked about his job at '*the Manor*' without the usual disparaging remarks about the owners.

Brock began dropping over to his parents' home a couple of times during the past week to start creating more comfort. One day he stayed for supper and all four family members worked together in the kitchen helping get the meal ready. They all shared what was going on in their lives and Brock found his interaction with his father was becoming more and more comfortable for both him and his father.

Brock smiled as he worked knowing his family was back together and wondered what Matthew would say when he told him about last night.

The sound of the doorbell woke Brock out of his daydream, and he went to the head of the stairs to make sure someone was there to answer it. He heard footsteps so he turned around to go back to work when he heard the door open and Andrew greet Matthew. He started down the staircase and met Matthew on the way up. "I'm glad you're here! I have so much to tell you about the Pflag meeting last night!"

Brock's excitement was a catalyst to Matthew's natural curiosity, "What happened? Why didn't you call me last night?"

"Slow down Matthew, I'll fill you in, but I need to set the stage." He continued with how the meeting went and how his father had spoken last night. They both had believed he wouldn't have participated like he hadn't in the first one he attended. Brock told him about his father telling the room about his counselling and openly sharing his feelings, perspectives, learnings and the apologies. He even talked about his father's comment about his own coming out.

Matthew could barely contain himself. "Wow, were you absolutely in shock when he spoke?"

"First of all, I was so shocked that he was actually talking to a group of people and secondly I couldn't believe the vulnerability that he showed. For a brief moment, a thought crossed my brain that someone must have replaced my father with an alien."

Matthew chuckled, "I can bet! Were you late getting out? I waited for your call, but I fell asleep."

"No, the meeting ended on time, but I wanted to talk to Mom about the change in Dad. By the time I got home, I didn't want to wake you. I only had a few minutes when I talked with you this morning and I really didn't want to tell you on the phone. I love seeing you excited like this. You're such a kid!"

"But a kid you really like, right?"

"A kid I really love!"

Chapter 37

Brock retrieved the sheets to make the bed in Mahogany Rest and he continued talking with Matthew as he worked.

As he looked for the fitted sheet, Brock said, "Now that Dad has accepted me and we're having family suppers, I was wondering if I could tell them you're my boyfriend. What do you think?"

"What do I think? I think this whole thing scares me a lot, but it also excites me. You actually want to tell your family that we're a couple. That's beyond fabulous!"

"Is that a yes?" Brock looked to Matthew for an answer.

"I want to say yes so much because that would make everything so real in one more way, but my head keeps coming back to my parents. Could we trust your parents to keep it to themselves?"

"I could talk to Mom and get her opinion. Of course, she would talk to Dad but with the new Dad we will probably get an okay."

Matthew reflected, "You're sounding iffy."

"We have no control over others, you know that. Here, help me make this bed." Brock threw out the sheet to give Matthew a corner and they worked together as they talked. "Can you think of another option?"

"No, but I'm thinking you already have one; what's going on in that mind of yours?"

"I don't want you to feel any pressure, but can we explore you coming out to your parents?" Brock used his doe-eyes as he looked at Matthew.

"I somehow knew you were going to bring that up. I am so freaking out right now, but I'm trying to show you that I'm cool. Is it working?"

Brock shook his head, "No, but take a few deep breaths to calm down. What scares you most?"

"When it comes to my parents, everything scares me! When I think of what you went through, I just get weak all over." Matthew confessed.

"So, let's assume they do everything that Dad did. If they kick you out, you could move in with me, so I would be your soft place to fall and you could live with me for as long as you wanted. But how will you deal with the family rejection and being disowned and all that that means?"

Matthew smiled at *'move in with me.'* and his mind got stuck there. "I need to process one thing at a time. I want to savour you saying that you would let me move into your place! You were a wonderful partner before we started this conversation, but now you're the best partner a guy could ever have! As for the rejection and being disowned, these are big things, but I had said I would come out when I went away to university and that was because I would have a place to live. If I now have a place to live, logically, I could potentially move the timing up a bit. Emotionally, just saying that, scares the bejesus out of me!"

They talked about it the rest of the afternoon and when Brock was finished for the day, they went back to his place and talked about it through supper.

Matthew was seriously considering what coming out would mean and as they talked, they were putting his coming out plan together and spelling out all the options. Having Brock's place to move into, made coming out as a very possible thing. "Should I come out sooner or later, in your opinion?"

"Matthew, coming out is a very personal journey. Only you should decide if you want to do it, if so, when and how to do it."

"Is there ever a wrong time to come out?"

"Think about it and let me know what you plan to do. I had Andrew and Gregory and it was a very emotional time for me. It is never easy no matter how much you plan."

"Let's watch something on Netflix and forget about it for tonight. I'll think about all that we've talked about and when I'm ready we can talk about it then."

"Okay, there is a great series that I want to start watching. I don't want you to feel any pressure from me, so we'll not talk about you coming out to your parents again until you to bring it up. Deal?"

Matthew smiled, "Deal!"

*****

Brock opened the door and was surprised to find his father standing there.

"Can I come in?" Grant asked.

Brock stepped aside and made a sweeping motion with one hand saying, "Dad you are always welcome in my home. Come on in! I just didn't think you would want to be here yet."

"I know I deserve that, but I want to share something with you. I think you are the right person to hear this story."

"Would you like a drink? I have coffee, tea, hot chocolate, pop or water."

"Water will be fine."

He got a jug out of the fridge and poured two glasses. "Let's go to the living room and sit."

After they seated, Grant started his story, "Brock, I have not been able to share this story with anyone, but my therapist and I thought you should be the first to hear it." He hesitated and then began, "When I was a boy........"

He laid the groundwork for the information he felt he had to share. He introduced the key players in his life: his cold, emotionally absent dad, his obedient, and 'loyal-to-her-husband' wife, the vulnerable young Grant who was craving attention, and the young, charismatic, emotionally present, and engaging Father Mike. He talked about the relationship he had with each and painted the picture of how he idolized Father Mike. As he spoke, he detailed why he thought his relationship with Father Mike had evolved. He explained the ten years of pure affection he carried for him and how he was blinded because he so badly wanted a dad who cared about him and how he thought Father Mike became his replacement dad. He spelled out the special one-on-one connection they shared in the First Aid room and how special he felt. Father Mike was proving to be the father his dad would never be.

Grant paused because he knew the next part of the story was going to be the hardest for him to share but he had made a commitment in his last therapy session to be vulnerable with Brock.

Brock recognized someone in pain and could only guess what story was going to be told. He remained quiet and let his father gather himself.

He started the next segment with, "Then one day......" and he laid open his darkest secrets for Brock to witness and understand. He shared the feelings, the actions, the decisions, the manipulation, and the betrayal. He spoke of the pain of realization and not wanting to believe he was being used. He explained the lost innocence and the unbidden trust and love he carried only to be pushed aside when he was no longer in favour or, at least, that is how he felt. As he detailed what had happened, tears flowed down his cheeks unchecked to pool on his collar. He talked about the horror of the moment he opened the door to the First Aid room and discovered Father Mike with Albert. He spoke of the hug the Bishop gave so he wouldn't see anything although he had already borne witness to the betrayal. He explained how Father Mike disappeared and he hadn't seen or heard from him since that day. He talked about the hurt of the lost trust and how he ached when he mourned the person he thought Father Mike was. He exposed all of his skeletons to the last bone and sat in an exhausted heap on the couch.

Brock was in a state of shock as he gathered his father's words into disbelief that quickly morphed into the horror of what a young boy had to endure. When his father stopped, Brock went over to him and they hugged. They held on to each other while tears of raw, unedited pain flowed freely.

"Dad, you carried this pain through your life without telling anyone?"

"I was so ashamed that I couldn't allow myself to share anything. I blamed myself and felt that I was somehow responsible. The fear you talked about in the Pflag meetings spoke to me in a way I never expected, and my therapy sessions helped me dislodge these hidden memories. I'm telling you today because I have realized that I hid behind all of my hateful statements so no one would guess what I had done. It became a natural and first-response reaction that coloured me in a negative light. I just couldn't let myself remember all of the abuse and the pain that came with it so I caused pain to others. Brock, I am so deeply ashamed of how I treated you. I should have been there to support you through all of those dark times where you had no place to turn. I should have been your safe place to turn. I know what it is like to have no one to talk to and I should have been the father you could depend on. I let you down. I am so sorry." He started crying and Brock held him until he calmed.

"Dad, I never knew you were suffering. How could you support me when you had no idea what support looked like? I forgive you."

"Thank you, son."

"What ever happened to Father Mike?"

"Father Mike was sent away. Where to and to do what, I don't know. I thought about finding him so I could tell him to his face how he hurt me. When I thought about it, I determined that it would just bring back everything I had struggled with most of my life, so I quickly dismissed the idea. Every time a story came on TV about abuse in the Catholic Church, I switched the channel. I needed to keep my memories buried so I could live my life."

"Did you ever get mad at the church?"

"No, I never did, I was mad at the person, Father Mike. I was also mad at me for allowing it to happen. He never really used physical force and because I would do anything he wanted, I blamed myself. My therapist reminded me that I was a child and didn't have the maturity to give consent. I logically understand that, but I'm still working on forgiving myself. When I focused my anger at Father Mike, I ignored the rest. Lately, I have discovered I'm angry at the Bishop for covering it up. After we caught them that day, my life was forever affected in negative ways and I wanted to get rid of the pain it caused so I buried the memories. With the help of my therapist, I am processing the messages that came out of everything that happened. The church has been coming to the forefront lately. I needed to understand where the people working in the church stop and the Church starts. I was always clear that it was Father Mike but now that I'm exploring the abuse, I see the church had a role in it. People put so much trust in the church and the priests were the church. They failed me like they failed the thousands of kids like me when they decided to keep the abuse hidden. I wonder how many other children were abused by Father Mike in the past thirty years because the church did nothing to stop it." He paused as if forming a question and then he spoke, "Did you ever wonder why we didn't force you to go to church?"

"Mackenzie and I have remarked on that over the years. You and Mom would go but you let us make up our own minds."

"I didn't want you to end up being abused by a paedophile, so I convinced your mom to allow you the freedom to make your own decisions. I was almost relieved when you didn't go but I couldn't tell that to your mom."

"Is that why you were so against gays and called them all paedophiles?"

"The short answer is yes. The long answer is that I thought Father Mike was gay and that is why he abused me. My therapist helped me understand that paedophiles are not necessarily gay. She tells me that paedophilia is a sickness, and it is completely separate from sexual orientation. I had equated gay people with paedophiles, and I lashed out about gay rights and gay marriage. It just didn't make sense to me that we, as a society, put an okay sticker on sexual abuse. That is how I was seeing it. Your mom and Mackenzie kept telling me I was ignorant and needed an education and they were right as much as I didn't want to admit it. I started my education and now I know Father Mike was definitely a paedophile and whether he was gay or not, I don't know. That was a big 'aha' moment for me."

"That explains so much, Dad."

"I'm glad you see that. I'm so sorry for all the pain I caused you and I want our family to heal and move on."

"Will you be telling Mom and Mackenzie?"

"Yes, they deserve to know. It'll be difficult for me, but I can do it. I would like to do it tomorrow after supper. What do you think?"

"Tomorrow, Matthew is joining us so maybe the next Sunday would be better."

"If he is going to be part of the family, maybe it is good that he will be there."

"What do you mean?"

"Brock, the way you look at him tells me there is more than friendship. Is he special or maybe even your boyfriend?"

"Yes, Dad, he is my boyfriend. We were going to tell the family tomorrow."

"Good for you. He is a wonderful young man."

"Thank you, Dad. Mackenzie knows so I need to tell Mom."

"She likes Matthew, I think she'll be happy for you." Grant stood. "I guess I had better get going. Thank you for being so understanding about all of this. You certainly didn't learn that trait from me."

Brock stood, walked his dad to the door and gave him a hug. "I have learned lots of things from you over the years. Thank you, Dad. I love you!"

Chapter 38

Matthew called Brock. "I know I have been silent over the past four days but coming out to my parents still scares me beyond belief! Now that I have said that, I have played it from every angle, and I think I'm ready. Before I make it definite, I want to talk. Can I come over?"

"You know you can come anytime."

"I love you! See you soon!"

Brock was finishing off the dishes when Matthew came in the back door. "I just met your father out in the yard, and he was in a great mood. We had a nice chat about school and what I was planning to do in the fall."

"Did you tell him that you were planning to come out to your parents and maybe that you were madly in love with his son?"

"Yeah, like that's going to happen; maybe someday. Do you ever think we'll be that free that we can be open everywhere?"

"Dad was here earlier, and we had a great talk. He guessed that you were special to me and asked if we were boyfriends. I told him we are and he congratulated us! Can you believe that?"

"Wow Brock that is amazing! We are out to your family!"

"Not quite all. I need to tell Mom, but I don't expect any issues with her. As for others, the only thing that's really stopping us is worrying about what other people will think. Once we get rid of that fear, we'll be free."

"Like Andrew and Gregory?"

"Yes, I think those two have total freedom to be who they are. I want that."

"So, that takes us right back to coming out to my parents."

"When you called, you said you were ready. What do you need to talk about?"

Matthew looked at Brock, "There are times in my thinking that it makes so much sense and I feel like I could walk into the room and tell them, but then my fear gets in the way and I climb back into the closet."

"Can you talk about what your fear is?"

"I think it's that I was brought up that they had the final say on my life and I don't know how to take it over. It's almost like fear of failure. What if I screw it up?"

"You won't screw it up. What are you concerned about?"

"Worst case is that they kill me."

"That isn't likely to happen, so I think it's safe to put that one aside."

"That was my attempt at making a joke, but I'm not feeling really funny right now. Getting disowned and losing my family would be devastating, but then I look at you and you lived through it. Will I live through it?"

"I don't see any reason why you shouldn't. Remember, I'm here to support you through everything, no matter what."

"I know and I love that you're so supportive and that you, not only lived through your worst-case scenario, but you are also now at a place where everything is good. When I think of that I want to go right home and come out!"

"Are you thinking tonight?"

"No, I want to get some of my things together while they are at church tomorrow and have them here in case they kick me out. Can you bring your car over and help me move some things?"

"Name the time and I'll be there. Are you packed?"

"I have the bags in my closet and plan to pack tonight. What if I chicken out; will you hate me?"

"This is on your schedule, if you change your mind, you can do it another day. There is no rush unless you make it so. For the record, I could never hate you!"

"Thank you for that. Can we spend some quality time together before I have to go home?"

"You're horny again, aren't you?"

"When am I not?"

*****

Matthew called Brock after his parents left for church. "Can you come over now?"

"Sure, I'll be right there! Did they accept that you weren't feeling well?"

"Very well; probably because my stomach was so upset that I threw up from stress so, in a weird way, I wasn't lying!"

Brock pulled his car up to the house and Matthew brought a bag out. "I have about three more if you could help."

Brock loaded the car and went back in the house for the last box. Before he left, he hugged Matthew and whispered into his ear, "Are you sure you're ready?"

"I'm as ready as I can get. I plan to tell them after lunch, so if they kick me out, I'll walk over to your place. If they don't, we may be talking awhile, so I'll let you know."

Brock pulled out a key and gave it to Matthew. "This is your key to use anytime you need it."

Matthew kissed Brock, "Thank you. Now get out before they come back."

Chapter 39

Matthew heard his parents arrive home and, as expected, his mother's footsteps were coming up the stairs. "How are you feeling?"

"So-so, but I haven't thrown up again."

"That's good. I'll heat up a bowl of the chicken soup I made yesterday. You can eat only the broth if it's too heavy on your stomach. Do you feel like coming down to the table?"

"I think I can do that."

"Come with me and I'll support you in case you get dizzy." Bonny, ever on guard, and Matthew made their way downstairs and out to the kitchen where Matthew took a seat."

Matthew's father, Doug, saw the soup being heated, "That was good soup, I'll have a bowl, too."

"I guess we'll all have soup."

Pretty soon the bowls were steaming on the table and everyone was sipping from their spoons. As they ate, his parents summarized the happening at church almost as if Matthew might be interested.

Matthew was playing his own narrative in his head and as his soup went down, his stress level went up. He considered aborting the coming out after every third or fourth spoonful but talked himself out of it each time. Finally, they all were nearing the end of their lunch. Matthew had zoned out and had no clue about what his parents were saying.

Matthew decided to bite the bullet, "Mom and Dad, I'm gay."

"You're what?" Doug asked.

"I'm gay."

Doug jumped in right on the end of his statement. "Don't say that! Why would you say something so horrible about yourself? If this is a sick joke you're trying to pull; we don't find it amusing at all!"

"This isn't a joke; I am attracted to men. It's only horrible if you tell yourself it's horrible. 'm quite relieved to be telling you because I have known for years. When I was a small child was attracted to men and I have never been attracted to a girl." Matthew explained.

Bonny joined in, "You're not gay, you're just confused. You're only eighteen; you haven't given yourself time to know who you are. Maybe you should get a girlfriend and try that before you decide."

"There is nothing to decide; I'm gay. Gee Mom, you make it sound like I need to test drive a different sexual orientation. I don't need to try out a girlfriend. This is me; I'm gay, 'm informed, well-adjusted and very happy. By the way, I also have a boyfriend."

Doug got into detective mode, "A boyfriend! Who is this person? Don't let him tell you who you are! You are a heterosexual, and this boyfriend has somehow convinced you to choose o be gay."

"Dad, it isn't a choice. When did you choose to be heterosexual?"

"I didn't have to choose."

"I didn't have to choose either, Dad; I'm gay. The only choice I have is to live a lie, which ou seem to be okay with as long as I pretend to be heterosexual. The trouble is I cannot pretend anymore. In my upbringing, you both have taught me a set of values and one of those alues is honesty. Would you rather I lie about who I am, or do you want me to live honestly? Gay is naturally who I am."

Doug's face morphed into shades of red, "There is nothing natural about being gay. God reated you heterosexual."

"Dad, if it occurs in nature; it's natural and God created it. There are lots of studies that ound there are hundreds of species of animals which engage in sexual activity with members f the same sex and have same-sex relationships; many for life. Some of the animals they tudied you have probably heard about like dolphins, penguins, bears, giraffes, and lizards to ame a few. God creates many sexual orientations; heterosexual, homosexual and bisexual are ome of the most understood, but there are others. If you want to go down that road, think bout this, God created me as a DNA combination between you and Mom and something 1 your DNA contributed to my sexual orientation of gay. I'm gay because I was born this vay, the same as I have white skin, blond hair, blue eyes, I'm six feet tall and have a larger than ormal nose, but you accept all of those attributes. I was also born gay and I want you to ccept it without question just like you accept the genetic combinations that produced the est of my attributes."

Doug moved to a new strategy, "Our Bible says homosexuality is wrong. Leviticus tells s that God sees it as an abomination."

"Leviticus tells us all sorts of things that you seem to ignore. It says that eating shellfish is an abomination and you can hardly wait to have a feed of lobster or eat the shrimp stir-fry that Mom makes because it's a family favourite. How do these abominations compare? Just because you like eating shellfish doesn't make it any less of an abomination, but you seem not to worry about it." His father was about to respond, and Matthew held up his hand. "You need to hear the rest, so please let me finish. So, let's explore other abominations that come from Leviticus such as it says we can own slaves which we would never do in today's world; I think you and Mom would agree we would see it as a bigger abomination than eating shellfish. It also states that men cannot be near women while they are on their period, but I spend all day at school with girls and they are the right age to have monthly periods. What about you, Mom? You work with men in your office every day and I don't see you missing a week of work each month. What gives?

The Bible also states that we should not plant different seeds in a field, so our backyard garden is in violation of the Bible yet we enjoy the vegetable garden and plant a variety of different seeds every year.

It also states the wearing of clothing of mixed fibres is prohibited, but we love our cotton polyester blends, but you seem okay with it and as a matter of fact, we stay away from all cotton because of the ironing issue.

What about approaching the altar of God with defective eyesight? You both wear glasses to church and you have participated in ceremonies and events at the altar. How do we accept that?

It is also forbidden in the Bible to cut your hair and all three of us feel so much better when we get a haircut. How can we feel good about ourselves when we go against the Bible?

Touching of the skin of a dead pig is unclean yet we have played in the back yard with a football and not worn gloves. Dad, you love watching it on TV; how can you enjoy the many violations of God's word that happen in just one game?

In Exodus, you're allowed to sell your daughter into slavery. Did I have a sister and you sold her?

It also states that anyone working on the Sabbath should be put to death, but we shop on Sundays where all those people are risking their lives."

His father had had enough, "You're being ridiculous, we're in modern times and most of those don't fit today's world."

"Am I really being ridiculous Dad or am I making sense. You cannot refute these things are in the Bible and you say they don't fit in today's world. You got it – that's exactly my point. If none of those fit, why does homosexuality fit? Only because you choose it to fit. Well, I ignore that archaic garbage along with the rest; I just don't see any of it being relevant today."

Bonny broke in, "But, it says you will burn in hell for all eternity. We love you and are concerned for your soul. Would you do counselling with our pastor? He can help you see your way out of being gay."

"Is that any more relevant than all of the things I brought out? That is the question you need to be asking. I don't think it is. Mom, would you say I'm an intelligent person, given that I almost always bring home an 'A' on every subject?"

"Yes, you're an 'A' student, but what has that got to do with you being gay?"

"When I was a young kid, I knew I was different and I have heard the hatred our so-called loving church spews about homosexuality from the pulpit, but I don't believe any of you really understand what homosexuality is. You ask if I would take counselling from your pastor. Why would I? His preaching tells me he is steeped in the evangelical attitude that homosexuality is against God, God hates gays, gays are immoral, are promiscuous, are paedophiles, people aren't born gay, it's a choice, and people can change back to heterosexuality along with any number of archaic, ignorant beliefs that are all false. Somewhere in the counselling, he would probably recommend reparative therapy or suggest I join an ex-gay program of some sort and both of those are simply garbage and bad news overall. Why would you want your child exposed to such an uninformed counsellor who could do a whole lot more psychological damage than being gay ever would?

I'm an intelligent and well-informed young man who has researched being gay for almost a decade now, ever since I could connect the negative statements to the difference that I felt inside me. I wanted to know who I was because I certainly wasn't any of the stereotypes that the pastor brought out in his hateful sermons. I have read and understood dozens of papers on homosexuality, what homosexuality is, where it comes from and what can be done about it. From all of that research, I'm very comfortable that any of the dire consequences of being gay, that the pastor preaches, are fictional and won't befall me. To sum up, no, I won't get counselling from your pastor. He uses his religion to bring out bigotry and isn't at all informed. Can you tell I have no respect for him or his religion? I believe in a loving God who accepts all people and I want to switch to a Christian church that practises how Jesus lived with non-judgmental love. I want a church that will accept me and when the time comes, will be happy to perform my marriage to my future husband."

Bonny spoke up, "I was hoping for grandchildren some day. Now I won't have a daughter-in-law or grandchildren."

"Mom, this isn't about you; it's about me being true to who I am and not living a lie. I haven't given children any thought, that will be years away, but lots of gay couples have children. Look at Neil Patrick Harris and his husband; they have two children. In this world, anything can happen if you don't buy into the ignorance that people spew to try to control how we live our lives."

Doug had composed himself after the onslaught of information Matthew brought out. "What about your AIDS or other sexually transmitted diseases?"

"Dad, you should have this concern whether I'm gay or straight. These are valid concerns for someone who isn't using safe-sex practices. Not using safe practices could result in spreading disease whether I have sex with a male or a female, and AIDS isn't restricted to gays. I certainly do not want to catch a disease of any kind, so I promise you I will be safe."

"Oh Matthew, you have just put a heavy load on our shoulders. It looks like we can't change your mind and you have more information than we do, so we need to read about and understand what you're facing. Can you share your research so we can start our education?"

"Wow, Dad, I thought you would kick me out and disown me. I even moved some of my stuff out just in case. There are lots of stories of kids who have to leave their home with nothing, and I wanted to hedge my bet."

"Son, we love you. When you were born your mother and I made a commitment to each other and to you to help you grow into a well-adjusted, responsible adult and it seems like we have been successful in that. Now the child is the teacher. We don't understand all of this yet, and it might take some time, but with your help, we will make our best effort to learn. Will you help us grow into well-informed, responsible parents?"

"I will. Gee, Mom and Dad, you're surprising me. This is nothing like I expected, but since it's going so well, will you be open to meeting my boyfriend?"

"Not just yet. Give us a while to digest all that we heard today and lick our wounds, but yes, if this person is important to you, we definitely want to meet him someday." Bonny smiled a cautious smile.

Chapter 40

Matthew texted Brock and explained how well things went and that he was coming over. When he walked in, Brock was waiting to hear his story, "Well, I have been dying to know what happened."

Matthew took him step-by-step through the whole process and how his parents responded, "It's nothing like I expected; they were actually very decent."

"So, you're saying it was nothing like mine, that figures. If I had to put money on it, I would have expected my parents would have taken it better than yours. I guess it goes to show you that we just do not know our parents as well as we think."

Brock called his mother and asked if his dad mentioned that Matthew was coming to supper. She said he hadn't but added, "He is just like a member of the family, so bring him along."

Brock ended the call and announced, "You're coming to supper and I am going to announce at supper that you are my boyfriend; mainly for Mom's benefit but I don't want her to think we left her to last so Dad said he wouldn't mention anything!"

Matthew called his mom and told her he was invited for supper and not to expect him home till later. After ending the call, he looked at Brock, "Are we ready for this?"

"This is anticlimactic to some of the things I have been through lately."

Matthew added, "After the fabulous day I have had so far, this is just the natural next step!"

*****

Brock and Matthew went over early so they would be able to help with dinner preparations. While his mother and father were catching up with Matthew, Brock said to Mackenzie,

"Why don't you and I set the table." He winked and gestured with his head to go into the dining room.

She narrowed her eyes wondering what this was about. "Sure, after you!"

They went for the china, silverware and crystal that had become the norm for any family gathering and as they were getting it out of the china cabinet she whispered, "What's up?"

"Matthew came out to his parents today and it went really well, so we can tell Mom and Dad we're a couple. I already told Dad, well, he actually guessed and asked me, so he knows but I want to announce it at supper to everyone, so Mom doesn't feel left out."

Mackenzie looked at him, "You never mentioned that he was going to come out to his parents. I have to hear that story."

They chatted side by side as they set the table, "I really didn't know until last evening and it was still up in the air as of this morning. It killed me to wait for him to let me know how it went, but it went well."

Grant walked into the room and saw them, "What are you two whispering about?"

Mackenzie was quick on her feet, "Just catching up on brother and sister things. Can you ask Mom if we need dessert forks or spoons?"

He went back into the kitchen and returned with the answer. "Forks; we're having blueberry pie."

Brock smacked his lips and moaned a little before saying, "I hope we have vanilla ice cream!"

His father was in sync with that thinking. "Me too, I'll ask."

There wasn't any so Grant asked if anyone wanted to go with him to the store, but no one took him up on his offer.

Matthew was still talking with their mother and Mackenzie needed to know, "Does Mom know this is happening tonight?"

"I don't know if Dad told her, but I am thinking he didn't. Our new, improved Dad is amazing me, and Mom will take this in her stride. At least that's what I keep telling myself."

Grant returned in time for supper to be placed on the table. Martha asked Grant to say the blessing. He bowed his head, "Dear God, please bless this food we are about to eat for we know there are people in this world who know terrible hunger. Bless us with the love we share for we know there are many people who feel unloved and bless us with the courage to face our challenges as we grow to be like you for we know many have lost their way. We ask this in your name, Amen. Let's eat!"

Everyone started passing the different serving bowls filled with vegetables, the rolls that Martha had made earlier in the day, and the platter of meat from one to another until each had what they wanted. As they ate, they talked.

Brock was waiting for the right moment, but he had no idea what that looked like, so, as plates were emptied and forks were set aside, he waited for a pause in the conversation. "Dad and Mom, I asked if Matthew could attend our family night for a special reason. I wanted to share with you both that we have been dating for the past six months. He is very special to me and I ask that you welcome him to our family."

The air was still. Grant stood, walked over to Matthew, and held out his hand. Matthew hesitated, but took his hand. Grant got him to his feet and gave him a big hug. "This is great news, welcome to the Matheson family!" He released him and as Martha and Mackenzie hugged Matthew, Grant went to Brock and gave him a tight hug. As he released, he winked before saying, "I'm happy that you have found someone special to share your life."

The hug fest concluded and when they were all seated, Martha announced, "This calls for a celebration; who wants blueberry pie?"

There were I dos around the table and Grant offered, "I'll get the pie and ice cream!"

Martha smiled at Grant's offer and waited for him to return. Brock got the dessert plates and Mackenzie got the ice cream scoop and knife. Slices were cut, ice cream heaped on, and everything went silent as each of them savoured the dessert.

As Grant swallowed a bite, he looked at Matthew and said, "Matthew, I've learned a lot in a short time and my intention isn't to do anything but celebrate you and Brock being boyfriends, but I need to know something I learned at Pflag; how out are you?"

"I'm not that out. I came out to my parents after lunch today and no one else knows but the people in this room and Andrew and Gregory; the people I can trust. I wanted my parents to know first so they didn't hear it from anyone but me."

"How did that go?"

"It went well. They are very religious, and I expected them to not accept my news, but they surprised me."

Martha joined in, "Isn't that wonderful; how fortunate you are!"

"Thank you. I gave them a lot to think about, so they do not know about Brock yet. They do know I have a boyfriend and they would like to meet him, but not until they digest this whole coming out news, so I can give them whatever time they need."

Grant spoke up, "I wish Brock could say the same about us, but he can't. Today, I'm ashamed of what I did, but I have learned a lot. If Brock would come out to us today, it would be a lot different. Then again, maybe we had to grow through that to get where we are now."

Matthew agreed, "I believe we all learn at our own speed. One thing I ask is that you please keep this to yourselves for now and we'll tell people as we feel comfortable."

Martha spoke up. "We understand. Getting to where we are today has been a challenge. We had to unlearn a lot of beliefs, perspectives and stereotypes that are just wrong, and it took a lot of education to get us to this point. May I suggest that your parents might enjoy the Pflag meetings?"

"I'll mention the meetings to them when I get home. I really thought I'd be kicked out, so I packed my things and Brock took them to his place. Now I need to move back in." He stopped and looked between Brock's mom and dad and continued, "I had attended Pflag meetings with Brock before Christmas and realize the good they do. I have stayed away this year because I wasn't out to you both and I felt your family needed to do the healing they needed without me there. I have decided that I'll be attending the upcoming meeting, so I'll be there with all of you."

The meal was over, and conversation moved on to lighter topics while the dishes were being done. Afterwards, they moved into the living room.

Grant cleared his throat and spoke, "I have something I agreed with my therapist that I need to share with all of you. I believe this will help explain some of my past behaviours. Matthew, you are now family, so I welcome you to hear this as well."

He started, "When I was a boy…"

He told his story leaving nothing out. As he spelled out the abuse, tears flowed but he ignored them and saw the horror on his family's faces. He talked about the day he and the Bishop opened the door and the aftermath. He explained how he coped with the pain and the eventual burying of the memories. He laid out the therapy work he was doing around the abuse and the progress he had made. He ended with, "I am so sorry that I caused all the pain for you over the past years and specifically the past six months all because I didn't deal with the abuse effectively. I thought I was managing very well but it recently became evident that I wasn't. I am sorry and promise to continue to do my work and come out of this a whole person. I am open to talking about this so please ask whatever questions you have. We are in this mess because I held things back, so please hold nothing back."

Martha, with tears in her eyes, went over to Grant and hugged him for long minutes and whispered loving words that only he could hear. When she released him, she said, "I am so proud of you."

Mackenzie was next and when Brock went to him, Grant pulled him to his side, so they were facing the room and he put his arm over his shoulder. He then announced to the room "I shared this with Brock yesterday after my therapy session because I had to apologize for how I treated him. Even though there is no excuse, I wanted him to understand what was behind all the hateful words I spewed." He turned to look at Brock, "Are we good?"

Brock smiled, "Yes Dad, we are good. I love you."

Grant hauled Brock into a hug.

*****

Brock and Matthew left the Matheson household and drove over to Matthew's home to return the things they had moved out earlier in the day. They were almost done when Bonny met Brock at the front door. "Hi Brock, how are you? We haven't seen you in a while."

"Hi Mrs. Erb. Yes, it has been a while. A lot has happened this winter and spring so I'll be glad when summer finally gets here. How are you?"

"I am tired tonight, and I am on my way to bed to read. I'm glad I got to see you."

"Nice to see you too. Enjoy your book! Bye." He said goodbye to Matthew as Bonny went upstairs.

As Matthew went to his room to unpack, a knock on the door made him pause. "Come in."

Bonny opened the door and whispered, "Matthew, would Brock be your boyfriend?"

Matthew smiled as big as his face would allow, "Yes Mom, he is my boyfriend."

"He is a wonderful young man; I'm thankful you have found someone of his calibre. Do his parents know he is gay?"

Matthew told her Brock's story.

"Disowning you would have killed me. I feel bad that he had to go through that, but I'll bet it made him that much stronger! Good night Matthew." She hugged him a little tighter and left the room.

Matthew texted Brock with one more bit of amazing news.

Chapter 41

Brock was rushing to math class and rounded the corner almost colliding with three guys who had a reputation of being viciously homophobic and were verbally attacking a thin boy with pink hair who was wearing wildly different clothing. In the commotion of averting the collision, Brock took in the pleading eyes of the student and questioned the trio, "What's going on here?"

Bart, the biggest of the three and always the ringleader in any bullying activity, responded, "This faggot thinks he can sashay into our school looking like that!"

"Leave him alone. What do you care what he wears or how he looks?" Brock questioned.

"This school is no place for the likes of this. What's it to you; when did you become a defender of the fags?"

Bart's words hit Brock like a slap across his face, "Just leave him alone and go to your next class." He lifted his math textbook and turned to leave, "I've got to get to math class."

Brock walked toward his class at the end of the hall, but just before entering he turned to check if the trio was still harassing the boy. They were; they had him up against the wall and were mussing his hair. His anger ignited, both at the trio for their injustice, but also at himself for being so cowardly. Flying under the radar had its challenges and he felt impotent to do more, but he had his own demons to deal with. The memory of the boy's pleading eyes haunted him all day.

Jeremy Saxton, the grade 11 student wouldn't have stood out much in Toronto where he had lived up until a month ago. His pink spiked hair, multiple piercings and a wardrobe that defied any description but unique brought a new meaning to flamboyant for Saint John. He loved his life in Toronto with its diverse culture and his group of eclectic friends but supported his single mother's decision to move when she secured her dream job and a chance to move back home to the Maritimes.

He was a top student and starting a new school near the end of grade eleven was never a concern, but the culture in Atlantic Canada was so different for him. He had a tight group of friends he hung with in Toronto and was seldom bullied there. Since starting at Queen Elizabeth High School, the bullying was relentless. He was shy and didn't have a chance to find new friends because he was constantly on the lookout for the three main bullies who caused him most of his grief. He began to plan different routes to get in or out of school, ways to get to class, and avoid, as much as possible, any situation which may call attention to him. His eccentric look and clothing were so much the norm for him and his friends in Toronto that he never entertained the possibility that changing things would help him fit into the student body.

Jeremy thought he would be able to transition successfully but grew to hate going to school and hid it from his mother. Before moving, they had always been financially strapped, and he would hear her crying at night after he had gone to bed. Her excitement when she got the news that she was getting a second interview was a joy for him to see and hoped she would get the job. They had narrowed the field down to her and one other applicant and she was so nervous when she went for the third and more comprehensive interview. That night she told him in minute detail all of what had happened and how well she thought she had done, but she would remember things she wished she had said and started doubting her chances.

They were eating supper one evening when she received the call telling her she had the job. She was so professional on the call, but when she ended it, she fist-pumped the air and did an erratic happy dance like nothing Jeremy had ever seen before. She explained why the job was her dream job, how it would improve their lives, and fulfil her dream of returning home, buying a small house, and having money to do things they hadn't been able to afford. She was so occupied with her good fortune that Jeremy was able to hide his reservations about leaving Toronto. He loved that his mother was happy; something he hadn't seen often enough in his life.

*****

Matthew met Brock at his locker, "Ready to head home?"

He was rifling through a stack of books, "I know the book I want is here, I just have to find it."

When he heard Brock's tone, Matthew became concerned, "You're off, what's up?"

"I'll tell you when we have fewer people around." Brock pulled a book out, "Here it is!" He locked up and they walked down the hall together.

Matthew knew that when Brock was troubled, he waited until they were not around others before bringing the issue into conversation, so he chatted about insignificant things that happened during the day just to make conversation.

"Guys, wait up." There was no mistaking Mackenzie's voice so they both stopped and turned around.

Matthew welcomed her when she caught up. "Hey Mackenzie, Brock had an off day, and he was just about to explain."

"Bro, what's up?"

Brock looked worried and he looked in all directions to make sure no one could hear. "Today I ran into Bart and his thugs bullying a guy, I've never seen before, about being gay and I made a less than stellar attempt to intervene. If it had been any other issue, I would have aggressively dealt with the bullies and walked away with the victim, but because he was gay, I failed the boy. He has pink hair and piercings; do either of you know him?"

Mackenzie spoke up, "That's Jeremy Saxton; he moved here from Toronto a month ago and he is in most of my classes. He seems shy and reserved and pretty well keeps to himself."

Brock looked tortured. "Probably because he is being bullied and doesn't know who to trust. I hate myself for not doing more. You had to see his eyes; they were screaming for me to help and I didn't. I can't get rid of that image."

Matthew joined in, "I don't like myself for doing this, but I have seen him around and went out of my way to avoid him because I didn't want people thinking I'm gay. You know, guilt by association. It's bad enough I was bullied for being a nerd, I don't want to have people thinking I'm gay as well."

Brock assessed Matthew's points, "But, we are gay; that makes it worse. We thought it was hard coming out to our families, but I think we made it harder on ourselves to be half out and still be in the closet in other areas of our life. What are we afraid of, anyway?"

Matthew spoke, "Brock, you have never been bullied and don't know how humiliating and demeaning it is. I have been bullied most of my school life and, that's what I was afraid of until you stepped in. I must admit that I still fear that you won't be around someday when a bully wants to use me as their target. It's not something I look forward to happening again."

Mackenzie broke up the pity party. "Okay guys, I hear you, but making yourselves feel bad isn't helping either of you, and it's definitely not helping Jeremy. Unless you're ready to come out full scale and take on the bullies of the school, this will be the status quo for the time being. I'm in the best position to help Jeremy. I have nothing that I'm protecting, so I'll befriend him on Monday and hang around with him at school. He will have me as an ally, and they wouldn't dare bully him while I'm there, I hope."

Matthew added, "And they had better not even think of messing with Brock Matheson's sister."

Chapter 42

Brock worked all Saturday morning cleaning, but Andrew and Gregory knew something was wrong with him. After the guests had left, they went up to help him with the rooms. There were four rooms to turnover and Brock had all the sheets and towels in the laundry room and both the washer and dryer were running. They found him making a bed in Cranberry Wine.

Gregory walked in first and put his hand on Brock's shoulder. "You don't seem your wonderfully joyous self today and when this happens, we become concerned. Do you want to talk about it?"

Brock turned around and they could see that his eyes were red and angry. "Guys, I'm feeling like shit and I cannot seem to shake it." He told them about the bullying incident and how Jeremy looked when he left. "Why couldn't I just say to hell with what people think about me and do the right thing? I do it with every other issue; why is gay such a hard thing on me? I'm not feeling particularly great about who I am today."

Andrew took Brock's hand and started tugging him out of the room. "Come with us to the family room and have a talk." After they were seated Andrew asked his opening question, "How are you feeling?"

Brock jumped right in, "I hate myself. I know there is a better person inside, but I did nothing like I normally would."

"Why do you hate yourself?" Andrew zeroed in on the emotion.

Brock shrugged, "I take pride in being able to support the kids who are being bullied. I'm almost always there when no one else would step up, but I wasn't there for Jeremy. You should have seen his eyes, he was pleading for my help, and I walked away. That doesn't make me feel good about myself."

Andrew pushed, "If this is important to you, why did you walk away?"

Brock worked hard to find the answer, but finally admitted, "I guess I was afraid they would tease me and insinuate that I was gay."

Andrew continued, "Why are you afraid?" He and Gregory watched Brock wrestle with the question to let him have the time he needed.

When he spoke, he sounded defeated, "I don't know. I realize I have no logical reason to be afraid, but why am I afraid; it doesn't make sense?"

Andrew leaned forward, "Think. Why doesn't it make sense?"

"Well, it doesn't make sense because I really have nothing to lose; I'm out to the important people in my life and I have already gone through being kicked out, so all of that is behind me and I have tons of money so I don't have to worry about my future. Logically, there is no reason, but something is going on inside me, so it has to be emotional. Doesn't it?"

"Let's explore that. Can you go the next level down to examine the emotion?"

"This is hard."

"It is always hard to uncover something we have hidden away."

"Well, I'm afraid of people at school knowing because I know what they say about others behind their backs. I guess I don't like the thought of them saying things about me."

"What kind of things do you imagine them saying that you wouldn't like?"

"I don't want to be called all the negative slurs that bigots use to talk about gay people."

"How do you feel about what people say about you?"

"Generally, pretty good because they are usually positive, but I wouldn't feel good if they were saying negative things."

"Would you say this is specifically about being gay?"

"Yes, all the other areas of my life I have done very well in but being gay."

"Do you feel that gay is inferior?"

Brock looked at Andrew as if he were looking through him. Andrew knew he had hit the spot, he just needed Brock to get there. After a few minutes of silent contemplation, Brock spoke up. "I guess I must, or I wouldn't be worried about what people think. Does this mean I'm homophobic?"

"I think we're discovering remnants of old teachings that are still anchored in your psyche." Andrew stopped and then asked, "May I share one of my favourite quotes with you? It comes from Eleanor Roosevelt, First Lady of the United States from way back. I personally find great wisdom in it."

Brock nodded, "I could use some wisdom right now."

"She said, '*No one can make you feel inferior without your consent.*'." He paused to let that sink in and then asked, "It speaks volumes to me and always has. What does it say to you?"

"I'm hearing the wisdom. What I get out of it is that no one can make me feel 'less-than' unless I choose to let them, and I always have the power to choose. That takes me back to when I was in a grade ten discussion group on the '*Seven Habits of Highly Effective People*'."

"Great, we always have the power to choose how we respond to anything that comes into our lives. Think about the character of someone who talks negatively about others behind their backs. Do you admire people like that?"

"No, not at all."

"Then, don't let the opinions of someone with a flawed character define who you are. Since you can't control what people say about you, how will you choose to react when it happens?"

Brock looked rejuvenated; a surge of positive energy swept across his whole being and he beamed, "I will choose to stay true to who I am and ignore what they are saying about me. People who know me won't believe them and I don't care about the others. I will choose not to give them any of my power!"

"That's a great attitude. Eleanor had another quote I connect to: '*You can often change your circumstances by changing your attitude.*' and that's what you just told me. Remember, bullies only have power over you when you give it to them."

"Thank you for helping me see my way through this. I was wallowing in the negative energy of my self-admonishment because of the fear. I'll work on ridding myself of the homophobia I still harbour and see being gay as a neutral in my life."

Gregory piped into the conversation, "We actually see being gay as a positive in so many ways and once you gain your freedom from the homophobia that holds you back, you will see it too."

"I hope so! Thank you, guys! I had better get back to work."

Brock was rising from the couch when Gregory asked another question, "Before you do, how is your valedictory address coming?"

"I gave it to the principal last week. They want to make sure they know what I'm going to say, so they ask it to be passed in at least two weeks before the ceremony. One more thing I needed to get out of the way."

"I know it was weighing on your mind, so I'm glad you passed it in."

"Me too! Thank you again. What would I do without you guys in my life?"

Andrew spoke up, "Hopefully you won't have to find out for many years. On a happy note, the legal work for the shelter is done and we completed the purchase of the lot. Now we can finalize the design and start getting this shelter built!"

Brock's eyes opened wide and a huge smile brightened his face. "This is wonderful news! I have been so busy with my life; the shelter has kind of taken a back seat."

"Not anymore! We have a ton of work to do to make it happen but for today, let's get this place in shape. The next guests are due to arrive in a couple of hours!"

Chapter 43

Mondays always have a different energy to start off with, but Brock could sense something wasn't right. Students were gathered and others were going from one group to the next. His curiosity was peaking when Mackenzie came running up to him.

"Did you hear about Jeremy?"

"No, what happened?"

"Rumour is he attempted suicide Friday night and he is in hospital."

Brock fell back onto the lockers with a loud metallic thud. Matthew rushed over to them, "You've heard?"

Mackenzie answered, "Jeremy?"

"Yes, Maddie's father was one of the first responders who answered the 911 call suppertime on Friday. She overheard him talking on the phone and figured out from the description that it must be Jeremy. She is the one who spread the news. I guess Jeremy had taken drugs with alcohol and his mother found him passed out when she arrived home from work."

Brock looked dazed and couldn't put any words together standing there shaking his head in mournful repetition.

Mackenzie knew what he was thinking, "Brock, it isn't your fault; you didn't bully him."

"I could have stopped it, but I didn't because I gave into fear." Brock's eyes were wide but filling as he spoke. "I was thinking only about me when I turned and walked away." He put his head down and went silent. Matthew and Mackenzie watched, and his pain was palpable. Brock raised his head and looked them in the eyes and stated, "I can't go to class today, I'm going home!"

Matthew and Mackenzie in unison, "We'll come with you."

As they walked, Brock was relentless in blaming himself for what happened because of his lack of courage.

Mackenzie was worried about his focusing too much on that act and tried to divert his mind. "We cannot go back and no amount of worry or concentrating on what should have happened will change or fix anything. Let's spend our energy on what can we do from this moment on, so this doesn't happen again."

"It was almost too late for Jeremy!" Brock exclaimed.

"But it isn't too late. Let's put our heads together and come up with something we can do. I found a lot of comfort with the 'It gets better' program and maybe we can look at that and see if we can come up with something." Matthew offered.

As they approached the corner of Germain Street, Brock took out his phone and dialled.

"Hi, Andrew, we need your guidance; Mackenzie, Matthew, and I are at the corner and wondering if you have time to talk with us?" His brow furrowed and then he smiled, "OK, we'll be right there." Brock looked at the others, "We're going to 'the Manor'."

They met the guys in the kitchen after Brock used his key to get in. They all got hugs and sat down. Gregory put a plate of assorted muffins in the centre of the table and, looking at Brock, spoke, "The guests we're waiting for just called and they are going to be an hour late, so we can chat here. To what do we owe this gathering?"

Brock filled them in on the suicide attempt. "It makes what we talked about Saturday so much more hurtful. I want to correct the situation if it isn't too late."

"Are you comfortable with visiting Jeremy?" Andrew asked.

Brock looked a little puzzled, "I guess, but what would I say, I don't even know him?"

"What would you want if you were in his situation?" Andrew asked.

Matthew chimed in, "I would want a friend. When I was being bullied, I was desperate for someone to be my friend and..." he looked at Brock, "you came into my life and what a great friend you are. Jeremy must feel so alone being new to the city."

"Being a friend is a good start. What else could you offer him?" Andrew was doing his drilling down and Brock felt the pressure, but nothing came to him.

They all stared at Andrew, but their minds were drawing blanks.

"Think. What do we all need?"

Mackenzie excitedly jumped in, "I think we all need to feel we belong, that we're accepted for who we are, and that we're listened to, heard, and understood."

Andrew looked at all three, "If everyone had those feelings, the world would be a much better place. Now, can you do those things for Jeremy?"

Mackenzie was first. "Yes, I can."

Matthew was speaking before she finished. "Yes, I can do this"

Brock smiled at the other two and spoke, "Yes I can, and it doesn't matter who sees me. Jeremy is more important than any fear I have!" He looked at Andrew and Gregory. "Thank you both for helping us get to this. I guess there is always something we can do for someone whether we know them or not."

*****

They were waiting at the information desk at the Saint John Regional Hospital after requesting a room number for Jeremy Saxton. The clerk had made a call and they were told to report to the nursing station in the Psychiatric Ward on the fourth floor.

The door was locked; they were buzzed in and went directly to the nurses' desk. They explained who they were and were told Jeremy's mother would be notified. If she were open to Jeremy having company, she would be out to talk to them.

A tall, slender woman with long dark hair entered the hallway from down the corridor and walked, with purpose in her step, toward the three. She cautiously asked, "Hi, I am Margo Saxton, Jeremy's mom. Are you here to see Jeremy?"

Brock responded, "Yes, we do not know him, but we're from Queen Elizabeth High and thought Jeremy needed some friends. I'm Brock Matheson, this is my sister Mackenzie and my boyfriend, Matthew Erb."

Matthew had been watching the mother's face, but when he heard '*boyfriend*' his head whipped toward Brock and caught his eye. Mrs. Saxton saw the reaction but responded, "It's nice to meet you Brock, Mackenzie and Matthew."

Brock saw the shock and spoke to Matthew, "Jeremy needs a community of gay people, so we need to come out to him." He just realized he may have outed Jeremy, so he addressed Mrs. Saxton, "We don't know, but assumed he was gay. Is he?"

"Heavens yes! He came out when he was thirteen and it was not a surprise to me then. What is a surprise is that he seemed so well-adjusted all along, but then he ends up in hospital; I missed the signs somehow. They sedated him Friday and Saturday nights, but when he woke Sunday morning, we had a deep conversation. I learned his life has been a living hell since we moved here, and he has been harassed and bullied every day; sometimes several times in one day. He thought the incidents would diminish, but they haven't, and he feels he has no one to turn to. If you're sincere about being his friends, I welcome you. If you would like to see him, follow me."

All three followed her down the hall and turned into room fifty-seven. In the bed by the window, Jeremy was lying on his back with his head turned toward the sun shining in on him. His mother spoke, "Jeremy, you have some visitors."

Jeremy turned his head and saw Brock first. "You, you're the one who stepped in on Friday when those three pigs were harassing me."

"Hi, I'm Brock Matheson, this is my boyfriend Matthew and..."

Jeremy jumped in mid-sentence, "You're gay? I mean, I've seen you around the school and never thought you could be gay!"

"Yes, and I did step in, but I could have done so much more. That's why we're here." He pointed to Mackenzie, "You may also recognize my sister, Mackenzie, from your classes."

"Hi, Matthew and Mackenzie, I recognize you both, but I didn't know your names."

Mackenzie opened up, "Friday night, Brock was feeling terrible for not stopping the bullies, so we were hatching a plan to become your friends. Brock and Matthew aren't out at school so Friday he didn't want to deflect any attention onto himself, but from what we talked about and what I have seen here today, I'm guessing that will be changing."

"Yes, Jeremy, you're the first outside of my support circle to know I'm gay because I let the fear of being exposed have power over me. Seeing you in so much pain Friday and me walking away just tore me apart. I've gotten a reputation of '*the defender of the marginalized*' and I have zero tolerance for bullying, but my fear caused me to turn a blind eye to what was happening to you even when the rest of my body told me differently. We're here to provide you a support circle and become your friends."

"Thank you. I had no one and now I have you three. Have a seat; I need to get to know my new friends!"

They stayed and talked for over two hours.

Mackenzie filled him in on her school life and the support she gave other gay people and of going to Pflag meetings with them.

Matthew gave him an overview of his parents and his being in the closet and how he and Brock got together.

Brock told him about his coming to terms with being gay and coming out over the past year. He recounted his parents kicking him out, their recent reconciliation, and where they currently stood.

Jeremy went last and told them about the acceptance he felt with his life in Toronto and how he was out and proud until he experienced the complete opposite in the conservative culture in Saint John. "I thought I was confident and courageous enough to deal with anything; I have a great mom and I'm sure it's because of her love and acceptance that I have strong self-esteem." He looked over at her and smiled. "...and with a wonderful mix of supportive friends; my life was good. Before moving here, I never really understood how someone could be the victim of a bully. Just rest on your self-esteem and don't buy into their bullshit. Sorry, Mom. What could they threaten me with; everyone knew or could at least guess that I was gay?" He paused and everyone waited for him to continue, "Over the weekend I have had a lot of time to think about what got me so low that I would attempt suicide. What I didn't realize about bullying is the constant harassment in little and big ways, in physical, verbal, and emotional ways they abuse your sense of who you are and psychologically wear you down so you lose sleep and your ability to recharge your batteries. In that worn-down state, I started questioning whether they were right, and my self-esteem didn't kick in to help me see my way out. It was like I was in a spiral and the further I went down, the harder it was for me to believe life was worth living. I gave up. I gave no thought to the pain I would cause my loved ones; I only focused on ending my pain." He looked at each of them, "I'm so glad you made the decision to be my support circle – thank you."

Brock handed Jeremy a piece of paper. "We need to be going, but this is the contact info for each of us. Jeremy, please send each of us a text with your contact information so we'll be connected."

"That's the first thing I'll do after you leave."

They all turned to leave, and Jeremy's mother walked out with them. "You can never know how much I prayed something would happen to help him and I feel my prayers have been answered in the three of you. Thank you!" She hugged each of them and stood by Jeremy's room watching as they disappeared down the hall and out the doors.

As they walked out of the hospital, Brock realized he was changed by the visit. "I think I finally know the message I need to give in my valedictory speech. I could use your help; are you with me?"

Matthew and Mackenzie said in unison, "I'm in!"

Chapter 44

True to their word, Brock, Matthew, and Mackenzie communicated with Jeremy and when he was released from hospital, they made plans to get him attending school with some sense of security. Mackenzie made plans to walk to school with him and meet up with Brock and Matthew at their lockers.

Heads turned and silence followed as students saw Jeremy and Mackenzie walk to Brock's locker. The silence was broken by whispers as Jeremy hugged Brock and Matthew.

"So far so good." Jeremy said loud enough for no one else to hear as he was finishing the hugs.

Brock cautioned, "Just go along with what we discussed, and everything will be alright." Mackenzie piped in, "Remember, you'll always have one of us to walk with until the school catches on that you are under the Matheson protective umbrella."

"OK, we should get to class." Matthew directed knowing they had all of the day's classes and who would walk with Jeremy all mapped out.

Mackenzie and Jeremy walked off to their first class all the while chatting about whatever came into their minds.

*****

Brock made his way to meet up with Jeremy at the planned rendezvous spot and, as he turned the corner, he saw that the three bullies were approaching Jeremy, so he quickened his step and intercepted Jeremy just as they arrived. Brock slid his arm around Jeremy's shoulder with, "Are you ready to go?" He then caught the eyes of the three and directed his words to Bart, the ringleader, like he wished he had before Jeremy attempted suicide. "Jeremy is now my friend, and you need to think long and hard before you even consider bullying him because if you do, you'll be dealing with a very unhappy me. Got it?"

"Got it." Bart mumbled before ambling off.

"That was easy." Jeremy expressed to Brock as they walked to the next class.

"When word gets around, they will not be bothering you again." As he dropped Jeremy off at his class, he suggested, "Mackenzie will walk with you and we'll all meet at my locker to walk home together."

"See you later! Oh, Brock, thanks for this!"

"Friends do this for friends!"

*****

On their walk home they reviewed how the day went and agreed, for the most part, it went well. Brock explained that the only mishap was with Bart but that had been short lived.

As they neared Queen's Square on their way home, Brock looked at Jeremy and announced, "I am having a pre-graduation gathering at my home this Sunday; will you come and bring your mom? Mackenzie and my parents are coming, and Matthew and his parents are coming. I just have to invite Andrew and Gregory from Mahogany Manor. I want to have everyone for a sit-down supper."

Jeremy responded, "I can come, and I know Mom hasn't developed her social life yet so I am sure she will come."

"Great, six o'clock Saturday night. Let me know tomorrow if she will come. Also, I need to know of any allergies or dislikes."

"I'll text you tonight."

Chapter 45

Martha, Grant and Mackenzie walked into the June Pflag meeting followed by Brock and Matthew. Every one of the Mathesons appeared a whole lot lighter than at any of the previous meetings. Each one greeted people they remembered and talked with a relaxed calmness they would never have associated with a Pflag meeting. As the time neared seven o'clock, everyone took their seats.

Andrew welcomed everyone and started the meeting. "Tonight, is the last meeting before the summer break. We have no meetings in July and August so the next meeting will be in September."

He worked through the preliminary administrative issues and the introductions and when Grant's turn came, he opened up, "My name is Grant and this is my third meeting. I am the father of a gay son. It is hard for me to believe I said that so easily because not too long ago I believed he wasn't gay but choosing to say he was gay. I've come a long way, but I have a way to go yet. I am looking forward to tonight's discussion and hope to learn more."

Andrew asked for topics.

Grant jumped right in, "I would like to discuss what causes homophobia."

Andrew recorded his suggestion.

Others offered several topics which Andrew recorded and were included in the prioritization. Grant's topic came out as the topic to be discussed first. Andrew introduced the topic for discussion by asking who would like to start.

Grant started talking to the room, "I am interested in where the roots of homophobia come from in our society. I was homophobic, and I may still be in smaller amounts, but I wonder what makes someone homophobic."

A woman, who introduced herself as Rosemary, added, "I think the way a person understands a religion can cause someone to be homophobic. I have seen the bible used to communicate hatred in God's name. Look at that small congregation from the States whose members go to events with signs that say, 'God Hates Fags.' If that isn't homophobia, nothing is!"

Redge offered, "When I am with a group of my friends and someone says something that is homophobic, we figure they are hiding being gay themselves. I have seen this several times where someone says horribly negative and hateful things and then later, come out as gay. I knew one guy who would write hateful things to the newspaper and that weekend would show up at a gay party and hook up with one of the guys. He is a big joke in the gay community, but the regular community would read his hatred, and some would see it as valid. He has major mental health issues!"

Brock spoke up, "What gets to me is when people feel that there is only one correct sexual orientation and all the others are wrong, evil, disgusting, sick, perverted, or any number of negative judgements they make. I really don't understand why people are homophobic, but it is quite common. What is it to people anyway? To them, there is no entertaining the idea that people are different and forget about them respecting that diversity. They use pure negative judgement. I find it to be very elitist thinking."

"I can understand someone being negative toward gays if that person was harmed by a gay person in some way. It could even cause that person to hate gays." Mary offered.

Matthew jumped in, "Sometimes these beliefs are passed down through the generations. If someone doesn't have the foresight to question those beliefs, they remain ignorant and pass them on. Some people just don't question what they are told and take it as fact."

A teenager named John added, "Some areas of the world have laws that outlaw gay behaviour with a penalty of death or imprisonment. There could be a cultural bias toward the attitudes that could put those laws on the books. Citizens of those countries could feel they have a legal right to hate gays. I think parts of Africa, the Middle East, and Russia, just to name a few, have such laws. Hell, homosexuality was only decriminalized in Canada in 1969."

The discussion was waning, and Grant joined in. "I see there are lots of things that could make someone homophobic. After examining my homophobia in therapy, I realized it was my belief that all gays are paedophiles. I hated what paedophiles did to kids, so I naturally hated all gays. I was sexually abused as a child by a priest and I went more than thirty years believing that he was gay. My therapist got me to understand that we know the priest was a paedophile, but we do not know his sexual orientation. So, for all these years I painted all of the LGBT community as paedophiles and they aren't. Paedophilia is a sickness and being gay is a sexual orientation."

Andrew sensed the winding down of that discussion and added, "Thank you for your insights. Gay issues being openly discussed in public is relatively new in our world, so there is a lot of misinformation and ignorance on many topics. One thing I would like to add to the homophobia discussion is that the belief that equates paedophilia with being gay is one that many ignorant people carry without ever educating themselves. When that belief goes unchecked, homophobia naturally exists. As in many things about the gay community, education is the way out of that ignorance.

Are there any other ideas you would like to share before we move to the next topic?" No one spoke up so he added, "Okay, let's move onto the topic of coming out...."

Chapter 46

Brock and Matthew worked throughout the afternoon to get things prepared for their first gathering in Brock's home. They had just finished showering and dressing and were discussing the final things they needed to do before everyone arrived.

Brock looked at Matthew, "How do you feel about telling your father that I am your boyfriend?"

"When I came out to them, I told them that I had a boyfriend and they had said they didn't want to know right away. Mom had guessed that night so I assumed she would tell him, but I don't know if she did."

"Then let's tell him ourselves. What do you think?"

Matthew's thoughts were miles away contemplating the idea when the doorbell rang. "I guess we could but before we do, let me see what Mom says."

Matthew's parents, Bonny and Doug Erb, arrived, "We came a little early like you said so we could have a tour of your home." Bonny said with eyes bright with anticipation.

They took them on a tour and Doug took a real interest in the house. He asked if he could see the basement. Brock took him down the basement stairs while Matthew stayed in the kitchen with his mother. "Mom, when you asked me about Brock being my boyfriend, did you mention it to Dad?"

"Things were so confusing that day, I chose not to and then it never came up after."

"Do you think we could tell him?"

"I can't tell you one way or another. I really don't know what he will do."

They heard voices getting clearer from the basement steps as Brock and Doug returned. Bonny decided to give Matthew alone time with Doug so she asked Brock, "You said you were going to redecorate the bedroom, can you show me what your plans are?" They disappeared down the hall leaving Matthew and his dad in the kitchen.

"Matthew, you said you had a boyfriend, and I was wondering if he is Brock."

"Yes, he is, Dad. I have been wanting to tell you but wasn't sure if you were ready."

"I was only concerned for you, but Brock is an upstanding young man I would be proud to welcome into our family. We should tell your mom."

"She already knows." Matthew continued, "She asked me the evening after I came out and she was glad when she found out too."

Brock and Bonny returned, and Doug went over and gave Brock a hug. "Matthew confirmed my suspicions about you being his boyfriend. Welcome to the family!"

Brock smiled, "Thank you" just as Mackenzie walked in followed by their parents. Introductions were made and they were chatting when the bell rang again.

Matthew opened the door to Jeremy and his mother. Brock showed both through the house and was explaining that this was his first party when the doorbell rang again. "That must be Andrew and Gregory, there is no one left to come. Matthew, can you get it?"

Andrew walked in. "Hey Brock, something smells absolutely scrumptious in here! I can hardly wait to try whatever you're serving!" He looked around, "Any chance we can get a tour?"

They returned to the kitchen and Brock continued, "And this is where we started. I am so glad you could make it."

"I am glad our guests were staying another night because we would have had a challenge to be here given our star employee wasn't available to help today." He winked as he faux-punched Brock's shoulder.

Final introductions were made all round and they chatted as Brock and Matthew circulated with a few appetizers and drinks.

*****

With the main course finished, conversation was coming from multiple directions and Brock smiled to himself that everyone was getting along so well and showing interest in the topics being discussed. Every so often, uproarious laughter broke out and prompted additional comments that kept it going. Brock thought '*Tonight is better than I expected.*'

After dessert, Martha tapped her knife to her glass to get everyone's attention. "Grant and I would like to invite everyone to our home after the graduation on Friday afternoon. We hope you can all attend."

There were nods all around the table with offers to bring food.

The guests all moved into the living room and continued chatting as they took their seats. The chatting grew louder and more animated" punctuated with laughter creating a real party atmosphere. Matthew smiled to Brock and whispered. "We did it!"

Chapter 47

Brock took the long walk to the podium and glanced to where he saw his family earlier. When he found Mackenzie, she winked. He then looked at Matthew and his smile was a beacon in the sea of graduates. He needed to concentrate on their love and support now to do what he was about to do. He took a sip of water and cleared his throat. The silence was deafening.

"Principal Harrington, members of the Faculty, family, friends, and fellow graduates, today is a day we have been waiting for through all of our years at school, but this is a mere stop on the road of our life's journey. After graduation, we will disperse and move out into the world seeking the life we think we want. I need each of you to ask yourselves, '*Am I ready?*' and really think about your answer."

He paused and looked at Mackenzie who gave him the nod; he knew she was with him. He looked to Matthew and he gave a thumbs up. As their eyes connected, a rush of emotion came over him with a force he didn't expect, and he took him a few long seconds to compose himself. "It is a great honour to have the opportunity to speak to you today, and over the past weeks, I have asked myself what I had to say that anyone would want to hear. We are all heading out into the unknown, for the most part, and the only certainty is that each of us will experience much change. Will it be the change that will lead to your success? A good friend is always saying, '*you cannot change something of which you're not aware.*' and today, as I speak, I want each of you to focus on becoming aware. I want each of you to think about how my words apply to you, to your future, and about realizing your full personal potential as a human being. If I can reach just one person today and they truly hear, understand, and digest the message, I will be happy." Brock paused and scanned the crowd. '*Have I lost them?*' he wondered for just a few seconds before he shook off the doubt, 'here goes'.

"When I speak about success, I am not talking about how much money you will earn, how fancy a home you will live in, how expensive a car you will drive, or the brand of the clothes you will wear; those are all things and, yes, some people depend on them to define who they are, but they have much to learn. I'm talking about the success of being completely comfortable with who you are. So many people get so wrapped up in what others' think. They spend time and money trying to achieve what others tell them they should be or should have. They don't realize who they are or what they want to do with their life. When your focus is to the external, you have bought into the superficial game. Only when you focus on the internal, who you really are, and know yourself, can you determine what you want in your life.

Throughout my talk today, I'm going to be challenging many accepted norms in our society and I want each of you to ask yourself *'Do they have to be the norms I will choose to define me?'.*" He paused and heard a commotion behind him. He turned his head and saw that Mr. Harrington had begun to rise from his seat. He expected this because the speech he was giving wasn't the one he passed in a few weeks ago. This was written with Mackenzie and Matthew after they returned from their hospital visit with Jeremy. Mrs. Maddox, the vice principal, was sitting beside Mr. Harrington and took his arm, tugging him back down to his seat while saying something to him as he returned to a sitting position.

"That isn't the speech he gave me to review and approve, I need to intervene!" Mr. Harrington said to Mrs. Maddox as he rose to say something to Brock.

She put a lock grip on his arm and murmured for only him to hear, "Charles, when has Brock ever done anything wrong or hurt anyone in the many years we have known him? I say let him do what he needs to do and I know it will be fine. Let's trust him." Mr. Harrington glared at her but settled down.

Brock saw that Mrs. Maddox had saved the day, composed himself, and continued.

"Throughout the years of high school, I have made it my mission to support those students who were being marginalized by others who felt they were not thin enough, not rich enough, not pretty enough, not smart enough, not the right skin colour or religion, and the list goes on. I befriended many of them when no one else would because I didn't have to worry about getting physically hurt. I used my being a big athletic guy as my shield when I challenged the bullies. Some of you nicknamed me the *'Gentle Giant'*. I was proud of that name and lived up to it for the most part. I know I failed in one big area because I never challenged strongly enough the bullying of gays. I never actively participated, but by doing little to nothing, I now know I participated.

Jeremy, one of our grade 11 students, has been relentlessly bullied since he started attending our fine school just short of two months ago and I witnessed some of that bullying personally. Two weeks ago, I rounded a corner and almost collided with three graduates who are sitting here tonight, and you know who you are. I heard the vicious slurs and what did I do? I feebly stepped in but didn't do all I could do to stop it and I hurried to get away. As I left, Jeremy's eyes pleaded with me to do something that I could easily have done, but I didn't. I spent the rest of that day and into the weekend regretting the decision to walk away and I think I'll regret it for the rest of my life.

Jeremy was different than the rest of the kids at school and he needed a friend as we all do. I could have been that friend, but I was afraid. Not of the physical blows that the three bullies could have inflicted on me, but of the emotional blows; the accusations they could have thrown at me. Sometimes there is more pain in words than in any physical punch. Sadly, when I walked away, I was selfish and thinking only of me.

Over the years I have let you know the Brock I felt safe with you knowing and that I felt you could accept, but I haven't been honest with you. To do that, I had to be honest with me first and that was something I avoided for a long time, but Jeremy has helped me come to terms with me. I am gay."

He paused to collect himself and couldn't look at anything but the podium. He swallowed hard. "Fear has a way of distorting reality, but I now know that gay doesn't define the whole person. I'm still the athlete who loves sports, I'm still a good student who is going to university next year, I'm still the concerned environmentalist, and I am still an avid recycler. I am still a son, a brother, a friend; I just happen to also be gay. For me, I was taught that being gay was something to be ashamed of and to hide and I was ashamed, and I hid. That shame created fear that someone would find me out and I would lose the life I know – my family, my friends, my world. It got in the way of my honesty in everything I did and as such, it affected everything in my life. I know why Jeremy attempted suicide. Every one of us needs to be accepted as part of a community, to belong and you bullies made him feel like he didn't belong. Shame on you! If he had been successful in his attempt, his death would be on your shoulders; all for what you call a little harmless fun. It isn't harmless – it is all harm. Good luck defining your success when you carry that burden through the rest of your lives."

Letting his words sink in, he reached for the glass of water, raised it to his lips and let the cool liquid first assault and then soothe his throat. He scanned the crowd. He saw furrowed brows of disbelief on some faces, shock on others, and tears on others, but Matthew and Mackenzie's faces were beaming with pride and he smiled in spite of himself. The air was still, and no sound existed in that moment.

"Over the past year, I have had the opportunity to challenge, within myself, the thoughts, perspectives and beliefs I had personally held that kept me hidden and fearful and ultimately less than I could be, but today I'm breaking free. As a wise friend once told me 'we teach people how to treat us' and I taught you that it's okay to say derogatory things about LGBT people when I put up with your bigotry and didn't speak up against it. I taught you that LGBT people deserve to be marginalized when I didn't challenge your behaviours against them. I taught you that you could devalue LGBT people when I didn't call you out for the hateful things you spouted. I taught you that I was with you because I remained silent. I gave you power to spread more of your hatred.

No more! I am not going to let people, who are flawed in their development, define who I am. Now, I'm being true to me. I'll be able to be successful in my life and not hesitate to help those people who will suffer under the ignorance, bigotry, and judgement from the lesser evolved bullies. I'm challenging each of you to examine the world in which you live, understand how you contribute to the harmony in our society, and change what needs to be changed so you can be your best self. Are you part of the problem or part of the solution?"

"As we head out into this vast world to create our lives and become contributing members of society, ask yourself who you are and what that means to how you will commit to living your life. Only through working on yourself and finding out who you are, will you achieve lifelong success."

"Thank you."

Brock gathered his papers as row after row of graduates stood and applauded him. He heard chairs scrape behind him and when he glanced back, he saw the entire faculty, including Mr. Harrington, standing, and applauding. He smiled, took one last drink of water, and walked from the stage.

Acknowledgments

Being a new author, I had tremendous support for my Journeys of Courage series. So many people helped make my introduction to being published a reality and I thank each one. If I achieve any measure of success, it comes from all of the effort, big or small, by so many willing to support me in this, my first endeavour.

Special thanks to my beta readers: Wendy Sully, D. S. Mack MacKenzie, Tony Crilley-Porter, May Matheson-Thomas, Ross Leavitt, Nicole Collins, Cecil Kerfont, George McCaffrey, and Julie Bunker for their dedication, commitment, and feedback, all of which helped create my final product.

I am forever grateful for the loyalty and commitment of my husband, Ross Leavitt. He has been my constant life supporter throughout our relationship, and he is my first go-to for almost anything I need to do, including this series. He was especially there for me from the first formative ideas to the series' completion and encouraged me every step of the way. Our morning walks proved to be the perfect opportunity to bounce ideas around and many of those ideas helped define the end story line.

I have some of the most intelligent, compassionate, and dedicated friends who contributed to this series in ways some of them may never know but they were an integral part of making this series come together. I hoist the spotlight on three of those friends who stand out in their contribution:

May Matheson-Thomas for her friendship, perseverance, and commitment to editing this story. We talked almost daily for hours and out of those conversations, our friendship grew, and the series came together.

D.S. Mack MacKenzie for his unending loyalty, his involvement in helping wherever he could, his encouragement, and his seemingly unending stream of creative ideas for getting this series out to the public. When this series goes to audio book, it will be his voice and energy that bring this series to life.

Bridget McGale for her artistic eye and level of professionalism in creating the cover and formatting the series. Without her I would have struggled to achieve getting this series published.

TAKING CONTROL

There comes a time when the past needs to be put to rest to move comfortably into the future…

In this third book in the Journeys of Courage series, Brock Matheson's family grows through the life changes that he had set in motion when he came out as gay. While still defining their new normal, family members and their friends find themselves in situations they would never have before imagined.

With his family back together, Brock experiences a new freedom living as an out gay man. While he and Matthew prepare for university, life becomes difficult with new challenges. Brock finds himself conflicted with his decision to be invisible as Andrew and Gregory push forth in building Mammie's legacy in the homeless shelter and Matthew finds himself dealing with advances from an admirer. Will their relationship hold?

Grant felt he had successfully dealt with the demons that had tormented his childhood when he acknowledged the sexual abuse by his parish priest. Through self exploration, he discovered those demons plagued his life since in ways he hadn't really understood. His revelations, first to himself in his therapy sessions and subsequently to his family and the Pflag support group, were what he thought he needed to stop his torment and put his life back on track. They weren't. He seeks answers for why Father Mike still haunts him, and his therapy sessions help him to confront the decisions that will change his life.

A church's congregation is challenged to be more open and welcoming. They struggle between relationships and scripture as Matthew's parents take on their church to change their stance on homosexuality.

New discoveries, different perspectives, changed attitudes, and a determination to conquer fears help the players take control of their lives.

CPSIA information can be obtained
at www.ICGtesting.com
Printed in the USA
LVHW091330030523
745942LV00003B/67